MAN IN BLACK

MAN IN BLACK

Johnny Cash

ZONDERVAN PUBLISHING HOUSE OF THE ZONDERVAN CORPORATION
GRAND RAPIDS, MICHIGAN 49506

CSB

THIS BOOK IS DEDICATED TO
EZRA J. CARTER
WHO TAUGHT ME TO LOVE THE WORD

Contents

"Let every man who commits his thoughts to the public take special care that nothing drop even incidental from his pen that can offend those who profess to believe in the Savior, so as to either stagger their faith or corrupt their hearts."

From *Life of Christ* by Rev. J. Fleetwood, 1837.

Personal Note

This book could best be called a "spiritual odyssey." More than anything else, I suppose, it is that.

Many times the secular press has reenacted on center stage the low and high points, and the changes which have come about, both in my personal and professional life.

Likewise, the religious press has rushed to print things which happened to me and quote comments I have made in interviews, comments I often wished I had taken more time to explain — and even to understand — myself.

I wrote nearly this entire book longhand on notebook paper over nine months' time, dipping into my memory-well almost daily to tell you honestly what I did, and what I said, and what I felt during the good and bad times of most all my forty-three years.

My special thanks to Peter E. Gillquist, who spent many days with me talking about my life, helping me to remember, questioning, advising, and finally reshaping the book into chapters, correcting my 1950 high school grammar along the way.

Thanks, too, to Marjorie Dold, who waded through my scratching and typed the first manuscript, and to Irene Gibbs, who retyped it six times as I changed and rewrote, altered and added-to.

> To friends and fans in the music world: my thanks to you for living this story with me as it unfolded.
>
> To any and all who seek: if only one person can be saved from the death of drugs, if only one person turns to God through the story which I tell, it will all have been worthwhile.
>
> To fellow Christians who feel they have failed and fear there is no hope: it is my promise that this book will show you there *is* hope.

Johnny Cash
Hendersonville, Tennessee   *May, 1975*

1 / **A Traveling Song**

"When do you think we'll be there?" June asked.

"Not much farther," I said.

We were doing a concert in Laramie and were driving there from Denver. The land surrounding us was mountainous — massive, rolling hills — and the sunset in the big sky up ahead was beautiful.

"Looks like songwriting time," June said.

"Don't know if we'd have time," I said. "By the way the land is layin', I think I'd be safe to say that just over this next hill we'll be in Laramie."

"There's your song," she said. "Why don't you make that *Over the Next Hill, We'll Be Home.*"

And so I did.

> By the way the land is laying,
> I think I'd be safe in saying,
> That over the next hill, we'll be home.
> It's a straight and narrow highway,
> No detours and no byways,
> And over the next hill, we'll be home.
>
> From the prophets I've been hearing,
> I would say the end is nearing,

For I see familiar landmarks all along.
By the dreams that I've been dreaming,
There will come a great redeeming,
And over the next hill, we'll be home.

By John R. Cash, © 1973 House of Cash, Inc.

I suppose I've written close to a thousand songs in the last twenty years, and there has really been no particular pattern they follow: love songs, work songs, songs about real people, songs about imaginary people and things, tragedy songs, and gospel songs.

In the last few years, however, I've been writing more gospel songs.

Having been to Israel three times, studying the life and words of Jesus, and on the third trip doing a film about Jesus, with His words always on my mind, I wrote a flood of songs, one of them being:

I heard on the radio, there's rumors of war,
People getting ready for battle,
And there may be just one more.
I heard about an earthquake and the toll it
took away.
These are the signs of the times
We're in today.

Matthew 24 is knocking at the door,
And there can't be too much more to come to
pass.
Matthew 24 is knocking at the door,
And today or one day more could be the last.

By John R. Cash, © 1973 House of Cash, Inc.

Driving on into Laramie that night, June and I discussed the songs I'd been writing.

"They aren't very commercial," I said.

"That doesn't matter," she said. "They have a message — something that will be meaningful to people."

"I have a feeling my record company would rather I'd be in prison than in church," I said. (There hadn't been too much enthusiasm over some of these songs when they'd been released.)

"Give them a little time," June encouraged. "When they realize it's your faith that makes you the man you are, they'll look at this side of you with a little more interest."

"It's a money game," I said. "A number-on-the-charts game. It doesn't matter to them, for the most part, what the subject of the song is, just so it sells. So — I'll just keep doing what I'm doing. I am what I am. Whatever I am."

When I introduced June Carter on stage that night in Laramie, that special magic happened in me. That vibrant personality and sweet smile lifted me back up at a point in the concert where I should begin to tire.

As we sang *Jackson*, our first duet, I realized more and more how important she was to me. Along with all the serious conversations I had with her, she also gave me a daily dose of joy and laughter.

She'd grind out the words:

> Yeah, go to Jackson,
> You big talkin' man;
> And I'll be waitin' in Jackson,
> Behind my Japan fan.

And the wink and the smile and the little twist she'd give worked their wonders on me.

> When they laugh at you in Jackson,
> Dancin' on the pony keg,
> Then I'll lead you 'round town like a scalded hound,
> With your tail tucked between your legs.

Then we sang a love song, and she gave me that look which says, "You know I mean every word of it." And the whole audience had to be aware of the love affair happening up on stage.

Sometimes when I'm on stage now — feeling so good, feeling so strong — sometimes right in the middle of a song my mind will flash back eight or ten years to other times when I sang the same song, but with a frenzy — frightened because I knew my audience could tell I wasn't "right."

I'd slur the words, or I'd miss a word. I'd try to smile, but the nervous twitch in my face kept the smile from coming. Sweat would be pouring out of me after just ten minutes. Then into the next song quickly, no conversation; just a hard cough between songs trying to dislodge something that wasn't really there — a throat parched dry from amphetamines and cigarettes.

My eyes were glued to the clock, and by the time the show was over I would have given every ounce of energy I had with no reserve, just muscle and bone. At least I thought I was muscle and bone. I was hard as a rock, what little of me there was left, but I realize now that the muscle and bone was actually muscle *spasm* and bone, and when the alcohol wore off, a bundle of raw, tense, nervous energy carried over on amphetamines.

As soon as the show was over, I'd burst into the dressing room in a rage, stomp my guitar or smash a hole in a door with my fist, striking out at something — anything.

Then alone in my room with the beer and amphetamines, I'd pace the floor all night trying to outwalk and outlast whatever demon was snapping at my heels.

About daylight I'd take "downers" to go to sleep, but by the time I got to sleep it would be time to pack and leave for the next city and the next concert.

There the cycle would be repeated over and over.

In October 1967 I weighed 161 pounds, and I'm six-foot-two. I was almost forty pounds underweight, and it wasn't because I couldn't afford to buy food. I was addicted to amphetamines and barbituates. And I don't mean "habituated" like some people call it to minimize their habit's severity; I mean addicted.

I can't think of a thing I wouldn't have done to get pills if my supply hadn't been plentiful. I had a lot of people to help me get them, and a couple of times in 1966 or '67 I was actually so far gone that I attempted to burglarize drugstores to get a large supply.

I became paranoid. I carried a gun, and I thought everyone was plotting against me. I trusted no one. I wrecked my car numerous times speeding away from someone who wasn't following me in the first place.

After a few times in jail, I began to tell myself that policemen were the enemy. If I saw a police car, I'd duck down a side street, then drive like mad through residential areas, narrowly missing innocent pedestrians. Why I didn't kill anyone, I don't know — or maybe I do know.

From time to time June and many others would talk to me about my condition and show their concern. But I usually ignored any such talk. I told them I'd change when I was ready.

It was a kind of "steeling" and "tempering" I was allowed to go through. The hard times, the torture and misery I put myself through made me know pain and gave me tolerance and compassion for other people's problems and understanding of their many differences and shortcomings. But the greatest lesson I learned was — God is love.

I see it now as a little part of the master plan for my life. Some people think I used to be tough and now I'm soft. The opposite is true. I used to be weaker and more vulnerable, erratic, unpredictable, even unapproachable by most.

Many of those around me for those seven years I took drugs expected me to die any day. Most of them gave up on me more than once. But I knew I wasn't going to die then. I was running from God and whatever He wanted me to do, but I knew I'd tire before He would, and I'd make the change before He gave up on me. And He never did. So I gave up, reached up, and He pulled me to my feet.

The change that came was a healing change, spiritually and physically, and with the change came peace, trust, confidence, and understanding.

Following a complete physical exam recently, the doctor said to me, "I'd say you're about twenty-five years old if I didn't know better."

"I am, doctor," I said.

There has always been a group of people that my friend Vince Matthews likes to call "Johnny Cash watchers." That is, friends and associates who grew up with me and my music in the fifties and sixties and who like to talk about what's wrong with Johnny Cash now.

These people are would-be producers, publishers, promoters, songwriters, and artists who have become a little frustrated with me in the last few years because of the change that has come about that they don't understand or don't like. They want me to be like I was. They want to hear me curse again. They want me to wear a black hat and wreck my car and fail to show up at concerts.

The thing they don't understand, though, is that if the change hadn't come about, there wouldn't be a Johnny Cash now.

I don't watch back much at the Johnny Cash watchers, but I love 'em for watching. I appreciate the concern — even the criticism. It's important for me to hear, and I always evaluate it when I hear it, good or bad.

They've stopped telling "the latest Johnny Cash story" in the honky-tonks and clubs in Nashville. Those old dirty deeds that had the gossip going have declined, and in their place is calculated purpose, direction, and joy. I'm enjoying myself.

Some like to say, "Johnny Cash got religion," and put me into a category out of their sphere. They pretend to hide their whiskey or marijuana when I walk into a dressing room or studio. Then they laugh.

The truth falls hard and heavy: If you're going to be a Christian, you're going to change. You're going to lose some old friends, not because you want to, but because you need to. You can't compromise some things. You have to draw the line daily — the line between what you were and what you're trying to be now — or you lose even their respect.

For years June's daily prayer for me has been that God would give me wisdom. One day recently after the blessing at the supper table, I said, "I appreciate the prayer, June, but I don't seem to be getting any wiser. As a matter of fact, I seem to be getting more evil and unwise."

She said, "You have a good collection of the sayings of the wisest man who ever lived right in your Bible." So I read Solomon's proverbs again, and I felt better.

But, hungry for the wisdom and truths that the Bible holds, and having no study guide to follow, I enrolled in a college correspondence Bible school. About twenty people in my church are taking the course, and they meet every Monday night to discuss the lessons. I'm not able to attend many classes because of my traveling, but I take my courses with me and mail my lessons in every two weeks. It's hard, digging out all the answers for myself, but it's much more rewarding that way. Those great spiritual truths manifest themselves like a fireworks display.

My reasons for the Bible study and theology courses are many. One reason is to satisfy my hunger for a deeper understanding, a richer knowledge, and a closer walk with the Lord. Another reason is my love for history and, after three trips to Israel, especially my love for the history of the Jews.

But mainly I feel that the studies are necessary for experiencing the spiritual growth I need so badly. I have learned that once you stand up on God's side, the words of wisdom He imparts through the Bible are the weapons you need everyday, whether you're a preacher or a guitar picker.

If the joy and fulfillment I feel from the things I'm learning in the Bible are any indication that I'm gleaning a little wisdom, too, then June's prayer might be getting answered.

For my story has a lot to do with God. An awfully lot.

2 / Jesus Was Our Savior – Cotton Was Our King

I don't believe a man ever lived who worked harder and was more dedicated to providing for his family than my father, Ray Cash.

Stories have been written about me where writers, in trying to lay out a rags to riches, poverty to plenty success story, have not exactly drawn a clear picture of our family economic conditions in the early thirties.

Such stories have always stirred up a fierce pride and anger in my parents. Never were they on welfare, and never did they ever need or accept handouts, even during the Depression. At every meal thanks was given to God who had provided them the strength to earn that table of food. And it wasn't ever an automatic "part of the meal prayer." It was a humble offering of gratitude.

When the Depression hit in '29, my daddy was one of the few men in Cleveland County, Arkansas, who could usually find work of some kind. He cut pulpwood, worked at sawmills and on the railroad — any way to make a living — which along with all the food and animals he raised not only fed us, but some of the more needy neighbors as well.

But by 1935 things were no better, and hearing of a

"New Deal" farming community that was opening up in
the flat, black delta land in northeast Arkansas, we moved
to a brand-new, five-room, white house off a gravel
road two-and-a-half miles from Dyess, Arkansas.

The community of Dyess sits on fourteen
thousand acres of cotton land. There were numbered
roads that ran through the town — sixteen roads in all. We
lived on Road Three.

Road One ran east and west out of the center of
town and was flanked by the businesses — a general
store, a service station, and a movie theater where you
could see Gene Autry on Saturday night. We had a
bank, but it burned in 1936, and nobody ever saw fit to build
it back. Even today the citizens will point out to you
where the bank used to be. And there was the Dyess Cafe.

I'm not sure they even built a church there at the
beginning. Dyess was one of President Roosevelt's
rehabilitation projects and was government run. Actually,
it was a socialistic setup with a co-op store and a co-op
cotton gin, the intention being that the farmers would share
any profits from the gin and the store.

I almost forgot the cannery, where the people of
the community would bring their produce or truck crops.
The cannery would take whatever you brought in, cook it,
can it, and then give you back eight out of ten cans.
They'd hold back two so the place could keep running. If
there was any extra money at the end of the year, the
farmers would get that back as well.

The Road Fifteen Church of God was in an old
schoolhouse. I don't have pleasant memories of the
church services my mother took me to at Road Fifteen
when I was a little boy. My mother was not a member
there — she had always been a Methodist — but she loved
to attend. The thing I remember most was fear. I didn't
understand it as worship then. I only knew it was some
place mama was making me go with her. The preacher

terrified me. He shouted and cried and gasped. The longer he preached, the louder he got and the more he gasped for breath.

He was a young man in an old, brown tweed suit with a necktie that I thought must be choking him to death, for he could get out only three or four words between breaths. I would count them. When he got to where he could shout only two words between breaths, I just knew he was going to die — or explode.

But the people were caught up in the fever. The preacher would walk into the congregation and grab someone up out of their seat, shouting, "Come to God! Repent!" And he'd lead them to the altar where they'd fall to their knees.

Then more would come until the altar was crowded with people, mostly women, crying and praying and shouting with hands raised.

The writhing on the floor, the moaning, the trembling, and the jerks they got into scared me even more. And the preacher standing over a woman lying on the floor sweating and shouting, "Hallelujah! Praise God, Praise God, Praise God!"

Then I can remember the tears when he said, "She's got the Holy Ghost!" My knuckles would be white as I held onto the seat in front of me watching all this.

At the time I could see no joy in what they were doing. I couldn't understand crying being the result of anything but suffering. I can still see my mother's look of joy and happiness each time we left that church. And by the time I was five or six years old, I didn't dread it so much. I went willingly.

The Church of God allowed all kinds of musical instruments, and they'd have guitar, mandolin, and banjo to accompany the singing. But as far as I was concerned, the service might as well have ended when the songs were over. Because it was the songs I was beginning to feel.

About this same time my father bought a battery radio from Sears Roebuck, and I discovered those songs I'd been hearing in church were being played over the radio. We'd listen to the country programs during the week, church programs on Sundays, and the "Grand Ole Opry" and "Supper-Time Frolics." We'd listen to WLW, Cincinnati; WJJD, Chicago; WSM, Nashville; WWVA, Wheeling, West Virginia; and XERL, Del Rio, Texas. I thought they were playing those songs just for me, and I'd glue my ear to that radio. They were singing songs like:

> Turn your radio on and listen to the music in the air,
> Turn your radio on and heaven's glory share,
> Turn your lights down low and listen to the Master's radio,
> Get in touch with God, turn your radio on.

By Albert E. Brumley, © 1938 Stamps-Baxter Music Co. Renewal © 1966 Stamps-Baxter Music and Printing Co. Used by permission.

And I found myself getting in touch with something beautiful. It may have been just guitar, bass, and drum, or guitar, bass, and banjo, but it was beautiful music to me. I can remember songs like *Vacation in Heaven.*

Those songs carried me away, and they gave me a taste of heavenly things.

We also went to a Church of God over on Road One, and the preacher over there scared me as bad as the other one did. I didn't realize it then, but those preachers were instilling the fear of God in me, which is an awfully important thing for a man to know.

I was hearing the gospel, and the gospel was doing its work. By the time I was ten or eleven years old, though I still hadn't reached what we called the "age of accountability," I knew there were two distinct ways to go in life. The people who had their hearts right — I recognized them as being different from the ones who were playing checkers over at the service station during the church service.

One night after a sermon about hell, fire, and damnation, I was walking home on a dark gravel road. Many times in the fall of the year when the grass was dry, there were grass fires and forest fires on that flat Arkansas land. That night I saw the bright red glow from a forest fire and thought to myself, "This is that hell I've been hearing about." I remember being scared. Or I remember getting wakened in the middle of the night and looking out the window to see the glow from a grass fire and really shivering with fright that it might be hell.

As time went by, the fear left me because I knew in my own mind that soon I would make my commitment. I knew that it was meant for me to be one of those receptive ones. Even at that age I knew the direction my life would take, and it would be to follow Him.

But my way of communicating with God as a boy (and often even now) was through the lyrics of a song. Like back then there was a song called *Telephone to Heaven.*

> Central's never busy, always on the line,
> You may hear from heaven almost any time,
> 'Tis a royal service, free for one and all,
> When you get in trouble, give this royal line a
>   call.
>
> Telephone to glory, oh what joy divine,
> I can feel the current moving on the line,
> Built by God the Father for His loved and own,
> You can talk to heaven on the royal telephone.
>
> By F. M. Lehman, © 1919.

So I didn't have the problem some people do who say, "I don't know how to pray." I used the songs to communicate with God. And boy, do some of them have spirit. The man who wrote *I'll Fly Away* knew he was going to fly away someday. You can feel it in the lyrics of the song.

> Some glad morning, when this life is o'er,
> I'll fly away,
> To a home on God's celestial shore,
> I'll fly away.
>
> I'll fly away, oh glory,
> I'll fly away,
> When I die, hallelujah bye and bye,
> I'll fly away.

To me, songs were the telephone to heaven, and I tied up the line quite a bit.

I am of Scottish descent. William Cash, a Scottish mariner, came to Westmoreland County, Virginia, in 1673, and there the Cash family lived for a hundred years. They settled in a county where a man named George Washington would be born sixty years later.

For two or three generations they lived in Amherst and Bedford Counties, Virginia, as planters and soldiers in the American Revolution.

In 1810, Moses Cash was one of the first settlers in Henry County, Georgia. The old Cash family homestead can still be seen there, though it is in ruins, as it has been since the Civil War.

Following the burning of Atlanta and the pillage and sacking of the plantations in that area, Reuben Cash put his family in an ox-drawn wagon, and in 1866 he homesteaded in Arkansas. Reuben had a son named William Henry Cash, named after William Cash and Henry County, Georgia. He was my grandfather.

Rev. William Henry Cash, a Baptist minister, and

his wife Rebecca had twelve children; their youngest
was Ray, my father.

A most interesting thing to me in the genealogy is
the copies of the family wills, all the way back to William
Cash. God is mentioned first and last in all of them. They
begin with, "In the name of God, Amen: I, William
Cash, do hereby bequeath . . . ," and they all end with,
"and in the hope and faith in the resurrection of our
Lord and Savior Jesus Christ, I, William Cash, do hereby
affix my seal. Amen."

I have good memories of my daddy when I was a
little boy. I always thought he was about the greatest
man I ever knew, and I still do.

My dad was a veteran of World War I, and I
remember how so many times he'd sit my brother Jack
and my sister Reba and me on his knees and tell us stories
about his exploits in France in 1918. And he'd sing us
songs like *Over There* and one about an Army mule called
Simon Slicker. And he'd laugh and slap us on the
bottom, and we'd climb all over him.

He had a shaving brush that had been given to him
by the Knights of Columbus in Paris, France, and when
he needed a shave he'd let me lather up his face sometimes.

Dad had a nickname for everybody he loved. Mine
was "Shoo-Doo." He still calls me that sometimes,
which is all right with me, 'cause it takes me back thirty-five
years; and whether or not the good old days were all
that good, it's nice remembering.

And then there was the wildcat. It was the winter
of 1937 and about half our land was still jungle, and that
wildcat had been after our chickens every night.

My dad slept in the chicken house, and about
midnight we all awoke to the sound of a shotgun blast.
Reba was three, I was five, and Jack was seven, and six
little feet hit the floor simultaneously. Mama had
already lit the kerosene light, and we ran to the back porch
where daddy had dragged up that dead wildcat.

"He won't eat any more of our chickens," said daddy, and there was that big cat — dead, his sharp teeth still grinning at us.

For a long time my daddy was the talk of the countryside. People would come to our house to see how Reba, Jack, and I could all three at once lay down on the hide of that big wildcat.

Daddy taught us many things, but a most important lesson was that hard work is good for you. At the age of four I was carrying water to my daddy and older brother Roy and sister Louise as they worked the cotton. At the age of ten I was working in the field, and Reba was carrying water.

We soon learned it was not only our obligation, but our privilege to help make the cotton crop. We worked, too, with the corn and garden vegetables. We fed and watered the animals, the two plow mules, the cow, and the pigs, and I can't remember anyone ever complaining.

The time we all looked forward to the whole year was picking time. We were paid for picking the cotton, and *Pickin' Time* was the only time we'd have any income from the crops.

> I got cotton in the bottom land.
> It's up and growin' and I got a good stand.
> My good wife and them kids of mine,
> Gonna get new shoes come pickin' time.
>
> It's hard to see by the coal oil light,
> And I turn it off pretty early at night.
> 'Cause a jug of coal oil costs a dime,
> But I stay up late come pickin' time.
>
> Last Sunday morning when they passed the hat,
> It was still nearly empty back where I sat.
> But the preacher smiled and said, "That's fine;
> The Lord'll wait till pickin' time."

I suppose no two boys in a family were ever closer to one another or loved each other more than me and my brother Jack.

About the time I was eleven years old, Jack, who was thirteen, informed us one day that he had been called to preach. He had been converted a year earlier and had spent a year studying the Bible. I remember Jack's Bible so well. It was a little, tiny thing — the complete Bible in very small print. Jack just about wore it out. He took it with him everywhere he went — to school, to work, to church, and he studied it by the hour.

He would sit up nights and read the Bible as late as my daddy would let him, while I sat up listening to the radio. Daddy would go to bed at 8:05 when the 8:00 news went off. Jack and I would get permission to stay up another hour, sometimes a little longer. He would sit at the table in the dining room with his Bible, and I'd sit by the radio in the living room. The later it got, the lower I had to turn the radio because I didn't want daddy to know I was still up. We didn't have any electricity, so there weren't any lights flooding the house. If there was a light at all, it would be a kerosene lamp at the table where Jack was reading.

But I can remember my daddy yelling from the bedroom, "Okay, boys, time to go to bed. You won't want to get up in the morning. Blow that light out. (It wasn't *turn* that light out; it was *blow* that light out.) Turn that radio off."

I'd turn it down a little and get my ear closer in. I had to hear those songs. Nothing in the world was as important to me as hearing those songs on that radio. The music carried me up above the mud, the work, and the hot sun.

Daddy tolerated quite a bit of my radio listening, and he was even more reluctant to yell at Jack to stop reading the Bible and go to bed because my dad had grown up hearing the gospel preached by his father and his uncles. He knew how important that Bible was to Jack, and Jack was encouraged in his Bible study. Mama and daddy were both proud of him.

There are incidents still related by some of the older people who live at Dyess that happened involving Jack and his religion.

Jack and I walked into the co-op store in Dyess one day, a store run by a man named Steele. Mr. Steele was a member of a sect who said they were the only ones who were right, the only ones going to heaven. (You've met those people.) Jack had always kind of tolerated Mr. Steele's ideas about such matters, and he always tried to avoid a discussion or argument with him.

We walked in that day, and Mr. Steele was behind the meat counter. Out of a clear blue sky he said, "Jack, you know if you don't belong to my church you're going to hell, don't you?"

And Jack — I'll never forget it as long as I live — he looked at Mr. Steele and he smiled and sang,

> Have you been to Jesus for the cleansing
>   power,
> Are you washed in the blood of the Lamb?
> Are you fully trusting in His grace this hour,
> Are you washed in the blood of the Lamb?"

Mr. Steele's face turned red; he got mad and threw his butcher knife down and turned his back. Jack and I walked out. And Jack just left him with those four lines from that song.

To this day I have not learned nor tried to understand much of the difference in church doctrine. The preacher whose theme is pet doctrine or denomination cannot hold my attention very long. In my travels to Europe, Asia, and Australia, many times I have

remembered and realized more fully that the gospel is
the only doctrine that really works, and it works for all men.

I'm sure denominations are important for bringing
a body of believers together and giving them strength and
motivation, but when this or that denomination begins to
feel or, still worse, begins to teach that their particular
interpretation of the Word opens the only door to heaven,
then I feel it's dangerous. True, such preaching may
convict some people and win them over. But how many
more nonbelievers are alienated and will shy away from
any further look at the plan of God?

Telling others is part of our faith all right, but the
way we live it speaks louder than we can say it. The
gospel of Christ must always be an open door with a
welcome sign for all.

Jack was the paperboy in Dyess. Everyday he
loaded his papers, the Memphis *Press-Scimitar,* in his
bicycle basket and delivered them to everybody in the
community. Besides his basket, he'd have a sackful on
his back when he started out his run. He learned to know
everybody in town, and everybody learned to love him.
He was really dependable. No matter what the weather
was, Jack considered it a personal obligation and a
challenge to deliver the papers to the subscribers.

Jack was an inspiration not only to the whole
community, but to me — like a beacon for me to look
back to as years went by. When a moral issue or decision
comes up, I put myself back to 1943 and say, "What
would Jack have thought about this situation?" There are
times I say, "Now what would Billy Graham think
about this?" But usually it's, "What would my brother
Jack do?"

Like that situation with Mr. Steele, when I saw the
love in Jack's eyes as he asked the man if he was washed
in the blood, and he stood smiling while he recited all four

lines of that song. Jack didn't waver. It was Mr. Steele who wilted. Jack walked away smiling. Smiling, not because he had overpowered a man who was trying to needle him, but because he had been successful in telling the gospel to that man.

For Jack there was the Bible. For me there were the songs.

In a world of cotton fields and hot sun, the gospel songs lifted my spirit. I think I was getting some of the same things out of those songs that Jack was getting out of the Bible. It was the same good news sent to me from another direction.

Jack was my protector; I was the skinny one, and he looked after me. We were always together, always laughing. He taught me all those things a big brother teaches a little brother he loves. There was nobody in the world as good and as wise and as strong as my big brother Jack.

There was only one time that in my eyes Jack fell off his pedestal, and it was probably one of the greatest lessons I've ever learned: all men are human; all men sin; all men will fall short of your expectations at one time or another.

The farms of Dyess were crisscrossed and bordered by drainage ditches. These ditches always contained a little water, even in the middle of summer, and in them lived crawfish, eels, garfish, and a deadly poisonous snake, the cottonmouth moccasin.

In the hot summer sun, the cottonmouths would crawl up on the willow limbs hanging over the ditches and sun themselves and sleep.

A favorite sport of ours was to cut a long willow pole and crawl quietly through the bushes until we were within reach of the snake, then swing the pole up and down and strike the snake before he had a chance to fall into the water.

One hot Saturday afternoon we had crawled quietly to within ten or twelve feet of one of the biggest cottonmouths I'd ever seen. Jack had the end of the pole in his hand.

I whispered, "He's a big one, Jack. Hit him hard."

Jack slowly rose to his feet and at the same time raised the pole and swung it down hard on the cottonmouth's back.

The tension of the moment made my heart pound in my ears. The size of the snake added to our fear, and as Jack hit the snake, he exploded excitedly, "Die, damn you!"

The snake did die, and I thought I was going to, too. I stared at Jack in shock. "You cussed," I said. "I didn't know you would cuss."

To me, the word "damn" was a bad word used by the checker players down at the filling station.

Jack tried to smile and couldn't. Then he tried to say he was sorry. "I didn't mean to," he said. "I said it before I thought."

"I never heard you cuss before," I repeated.

"I won't any more," he said. "You'll never hear it from me again. OK?"

"OK," I said. And I didn't.

I think it bothered Jack that he had come down a notch or two in my estimation. He told me later he had asked God's forgiveness, and again he was all right in my eyes. Because he knew his influence over me had been temporarily endangered, he made it a point to heal the wound.

3 / Just As I Am

I was twelve years old on February 26, 1944. I was fast becoming a young man. My brother Jack realized it, and so did my parents.

Jack would witness to other people, but there was this funny thing in his relationship with me. I don't think he ever tried to talk religion to me or make it a point to try to tell me about salvation. He and I were so close that I'm sure he knew I was seeing it in him, for I admired him and looked up to him. He became a model — my symbol of goodness and strength.

Up until then, I had not felt a need to take a stand one way or another. That is, not until a revival came to the First Baptist Church in Dyess, a two-week revival, and I went every night.

It was a fairly large church for a small town like Dyess — probably seated five hundred. I remember the hard oak benches and the small amounts of oily sawdust on the floor to keep the dust down when they swept. There were the little brass chandeliers with four naked light bulbs and the windows wide-open to let in fresh air.

Behind the pulpit was a baptistry which was rarely used, except in winter, since Dyess was near the

Tyronza River, a small river not over thirty or forty feet wide at its broadest point.

A half-mile from the church was our old swimming hole which we called the "blue hole." It was a deep place in the river, and the trail you took to reach it ran through thickets of cottonwood and willow.

In the summertime I saw many Sunday baptizings at the blue hole. We'd always respectfully stop our swimming and horseplay and stand by and watch while the baptism services were performed. All the churches for miles around used the blue hole, and I often thought that spot on the Tyronza River must look just like the Jordan.

The first time I was under what I call "conviction" was one night at that revival after I'd just turned twelve. I listened carefully to the sermon. Then the invitation song began; I remember it well — *Just As I Am.*

As the people sang, I began to get miserable and twitchy and nervous. I wanted out of that church. As the song kept on flowing, I started thinking of all of those songs I'd been hearing at home on the radio and how they were pointing out the direction for me to turn right then. It was time to make a move. Either get up and turn around and walk out of the church, or answer the call and go down to the altar and give the preacher my hand, as he was asking us to do, and by so doing make a public show of repentance and acceptance of Jesus as Lord and Savior.

In the Church of God, I had heard it proclaimed a little more fervently, maybe with a little more emotion, but in neither church was there any evident avenue of compromise. Jesus Christ was preached as the one and only way.

It was not that I'd been such a bad boy. It was just that the right way and the wrong way had been laid down to me so surely by my parents.

And I had read so much of what was right and wrong into the things I'd experienced with my brother Jack.

The necessity of my making a choice was inevitable. If I did not accept Christ, I was rejecting Him, and I knew who Jesus Christ was and why He'd come. From the time I could talk and understand, I'd been told that Jesus Christ was the Sacrificial Lamb of God whose death was for my atonement, my redemption. I understood, and I believed. I needed Him as my Savior in order to become an heir of heaven.

Jack was up on the front row holding his Bible, his eyes closed, singing,

Just as I am, without one plea,
But that Thy blood was shed for me,
And that Thou bidd'st me come to Thee,
O Lamb of God, I come, I come!

I finally got up the courage to step out of that pew, walk down the aisle, and take the preacher's hand. There was not any big burst of shouting or fireworks, but a beautiful peace came over me that night. And a relief that I had stepped out and chosen the way that had been pointed out to me all those years.

It was something which happened so naturally for me that it was like a birthday rolling around. It was a milestone in my life, something that was planned for me to do all along. I'd finally reached that time, that time I'd always known would come. It wasn't like a drunkard's conversion or that of a long-time-gone sinner. It was the surrender of a young boy who had reached the age of moral and spiritual accountability. This was the "direction choosing time" of my life.

I felt brand-new, born again, as I knelt quietly at the altar with the other people who had come, and I left the church feeling awfully good that night, feeling joy and relief at having made my decision.

The stand I would take in 1971 at Evangel Temple in Nashville, twenty-seven years later, and the changes that would come about then would be a restoration of the joy of my salvation that I had experienced at age twelve. But more than that, it would be a complete returning to God, a total submission to His will for my life.

I couldn't know at age twelve that every day is a brand-new mountain, and though you might *feel* close to heaven today, tomorrow you can be down in the lowest valley. I would need a lot of feeding, nourishing, teaching, and growing, and a lot of years would pass before I'd realize it takes a lot of faith to walk daily with Jesus Christ. I never dreamed I'd ever go through a long period of running from Him — never denial, but lots of running.

That day in early 1944, I felt a new closeness to my brother Jack. What a strange thing that was. You know, it was like suddenly, as close as Jack and I were and as much as we had in common being brothers and all, now we were *really* brothers. Really close.

I mean, it was like getting a brand-new brother. I didn't put it into those words; I didn't say it that way. But it was like he and I were suddenly equals. No longer was I just the little brother who had to look up to him for every morsel of wisdom or advice. He wasn't just my big brother Jack any more. I stood shoulder to shoulder with him now. I really had something in common with him. Jack and I could walk like this forever — children of God.

4 / **Fork in the Road**

I have no opinion on premonitions. There are those who say they experience, from time to time, the feeling that "something's going to happen." What that sensation is, I really don't know. But I think my brother Jack did.

On May 12, 1944, a Saturday morning, Jack was going to work at the school workshop. I was going fishing in one of the larger drainage ditches that ran through Dyess, a ditch which was more like a river. I had asked Jack to go with me.

It was hard times. The family financial situation was bad. Jack was making three dollars for a Saturday's work at the workshop cutting fence posts and cleaning up the bushes and the weeds around the agriculture shop. Daddy was plowing in the cotton fields from sunup to sundown, six days a week.

Before we left home that morning, I remember Jack stood in the middle of the living room floor with his hand on a kitchen chair and spun it around and around and around. I was out on the front porch waiting for him with my fishing pole and crayfish bait I'd raked out of the ditch. I kept calling inside, "Why don't you come go fishing with me?"

It was a beautiful, warm May morning in Arkansas. The lush black dirt was growing not only good cotton we would be hoeing, plowing, and picking, but a few watermelons we might sell out at the mailbox to make enough money to go to the movies on Saturday night.

Jack and I had been to the movies together many times at the Dyess Theater which then was at the school theater. Often Jack and I had roasted peanuts and taken them to the theater, hoping to sell enough to the people going in so that we might go in, too. Sometimes we did, and sometimes we didn't.

But this morning I wanted Jack to go fishing with me.

"No, I've got to go to work today because three dollars will help a lot," he answered, spinning the chair.

I said, "Well, why don't you come on then, and I'll walk part of the way with you? It's a mile before I turn off for where I'm going fishing."

And he said, "I don't know. I just don't feel like I should go to work today."

"Well, why don't you go fishing with me then?"

"Because I need to make that three dollars."

Mama interrupted. "Why don't you feel like you should go, son?"

He said, "Well, I feel like something is going to happen, and I don't know what it is."

And she said, "Then please don't go."

"Mama, I've gotta go," he said. "We need the money I can make."

He started out the door, but turned around and went back into the room. He took that chair again and spun it around like a top. Killing time. Fooling around. I knew we were late if he was going to work, and I was anxious to get going myself. But he kept on killing time.

He put the chair down and walked back through the house, then into his bedroom. He sat down and read his Bible. A moment later he came back into the living room, grabbed the chair, and started kidding with me.

At the time, Warner Brothers' cartoons were very popular. He started imitating Bugs Bunny while he spun that chair around, saying, "What's up, doc? What's up, doc?"

I kept trying to get him out of the house. "Come on and let's go fishing."

He finally did leave with me, and for the entire mile we walked together I kept begging him not to go to work but to come on fishing. I had the feeling something wasn't right, too, because it was a forced kind of thing he was doing — the imitation of all the cartoon characters. It wasn't like Jack to clown around. I'd never seen him like that before in my life.

So I kept after him. "Jack, why don't you please go fishing with me?"

He'd say, "What's up, doc?"

We got to the fork in the road where I had to turn off. I went to the left, and he walked straight ahead toward the school. As long as I could see him, which was for about half a mile, he was yelling back at me imitating Bugs Bunny and Porky Pig, waving his hands. When we got to where we couldn't hear each other, he still was walking backwards down the road waving his arms at me.

I don't think I got even one bite that day. About noon I came back from the ditch, walking up the road with my fishing pole in my hand. It was hot and humid. Heading for home, I reached the place where I had left Jack about two hours earlier. And coming down the road in an A-model Ford came our preacher and my daddy. When I saw daddy, I knew something was wrong. The preacher pulled over and stopped the car.

"Throw away your fishin' pole and get in," daddy said.

I didn't even ask what was the matter, but I knew it concerned Jack, for they were coming from town.

Finally my daddy managed to say, "Jack's been hurt awfully bad."

The preacher never said a word. And I didn't ask another question. I knew it was terrible. I'd never seen daddy like that.

We stopped at the house, got out of the car, and daddy took a brown paper sack — it was soaked in blood — out of the back seat and said, "Come out to the smokehouse, J. R. I want to show you."

We went out back. I still hadn't said a word, and he didn't say anything else. He took Jack's pants and shirt and laid them on the floor of the smokehouse.

I remember the smell of hickory smoke out there that day. We smoked and sometimes sugar-cured the hams, bacon, and pork shoulders from the hogs we'd kill in the winter. Just a little pile of hickory chips smoldering in a pan for a few days in the smokehouse and the bacon would be hickory-flavored.

Dad laid my brother's khaki pants out on the floor with his belt and khaki shirt and a pair of brown shoes. The pants and shirt were cut from the bottom of the rib cage down to the pelvis, and the belt was sliced in two.

"He was cutting fence posts, and one got tangled up in the swinging saw and pulled him into it — jerked him in. He fell across the big table saw."

It was the first time and the only time I've ever seen my daddy cry. "We're gonna lose him, J. R.," he said.

I remember stumbling out of the smokehouse, weak and trembling. I sank down on the woodpile; I couldn't stand. I knew Jack would die.

The preacher took us back down to Dyess Center, but I don't remember anything he said. I'm sure he must have tried to give some word of consolation, but there was nothing that could have been said at that particular time.

There was a well-equipped, thirty-two-bed hospital in town with a fine doctor named Dr. Hollingsworth. He had a little gray at his temples, wore rimless glasses, and hummed all the time. The thing I remember most about Dr. Hollingsworth was the way he hummed. He didn't hum anything in particular; he just hummed.

The preacher stopped the A-model Ford in front of the hospital, and my daddy said, "I know you won't be able to see him or talk with him now because he's still unconscious."

The doctor estimated it would be a six-to-eight-hour operation with all there was to do — if Jack stayed alive that long. The internal damage was beyond repair. When the surgery was over, Dr. Hollingsworth told us, "Well, I just have to give it to you straight. There's no chance for him. None whatsoever."

He didn't expect Jack to live through the day. But the next morning Jack was alive and feeling better. Though there was a little rise of hope, everybody knew it was a false hope.

We all went to Sunday church the next morning. It seemed like an eternity had passed since noon the day before. Everybody in the family had been up all night.

Word had gone out to my brother Roy to come home, and to my sister Louise who was living at Osceola, Arkansas, at the time. They were told that Jack couldn't last.

The church had special prayer for Jack, and the place was packed. Many who'd never been were there that day. Even Mr. Steele was there. All those people Jack had delivered papers to had loved him so, and they knew it was his church. What the service was all about that day was prayer for Jack Cash.

I had gone into his hospital room before church that morning and tried to talk to him. But that joking Jack I'd left at the fork in the road the morning before was nowhere in sight. He didn't even look at me when I walked in. And as the years went by, that was one thing I never could understand — why Jack didn't look at me, and why he didn't have anything to say to me that Sunday morning in his hospital room. He was sitting there talking to my mother, and I don't remember anything they said except my mama showed me his hands and said, "They worked so hard on the operation on his stomach that they've neglected to bandage up his fingers, and two of his fingers were badly cut." Mama had just bandaged them herself.

Jack was wide-awake and apparently wasn't feeling any pain. I didn't know it then, but they had him on morphine.

That was one of the two times I remember Jack being conscious during the next week. The other time was later on in the week when I went into his room. I think it was Wednesday. He was reading a letter from Mrs. Williams, a schoolteacher who had been at Dyess and later left there. He also had a letter from a girl he had been "going steady" with. Those two were talking like they were twenty-one years old. I mean, he was going to be a preacher, and she wanted to be a preacher's wife. They were both so sure. She was strong in her faith like he was and was trying to encourage him and was reminding him that if he had to go, he was a child of God and everything was going to be all right. But Jack seemed not the least bit concerned about his own condition.

He still didn't have anything to say to me. He knew he didn't need to. It was like he was saying by *not* talking to me, "There's no need telling you about what's going to happen because you know I'm going. Any time now, you're going to learn to live without me, so start learning now."

At Wednesday night prayer meeting — a special prayer meeting for Jack called by a Baptist preacher who lived down on Road Fifteen — the whole community turned out again for special prayer. His condition had wavered — it had gone up and down. He had times when he felt strong, and mama said he'd lie in bed and laugh about things that had happened in the past. Then he'd have times when he'd lapse into a coma.

Saturday night the doctor told us that Jack had blood poisoning. Gangrene had set in, and Dr. Hollingsworth said Jack could go any hour. So the family gathered around his bed, and I remember there was a lot of crying and a lot of praying. Jack was still in a coma. He didn't know any of us were there.

Along about midnight he started hallucinating and talking to my daddy. He mentioned the crops and the fields of cotton and that we had to get the weeds out of the cotton. "If it keeps on raining, we won't get back in the fields, daddy. We must get the crab grass out if we're gonna raise any cotton this year, if we're gonna have anything this winter."

And then he'd lapse back into a coma for awhile, then go back into hallucinating. He'd be plowing with the mules and yelling at them. They were plowing up the cotton. He'd shout, "Open the gate! Open the gate!" And then he'd be quiet for awhile.

At about 4:00 Sunday morning I went into an empty room there in the hospital to go to sleep. At 6:00 I heard somebody praying, and it woke me up. It was my daddy on his knees at the bed across the room from me, praying and asking God for the life of his son. I knew the time had come. I could hear it in my daddy's prayer.

I sat up on the side of the bed, and I think it was the first time my daddy realized I was in the room. "J. R.," he said, "you better come on in Jack's room. He's dying."

I went in there, and my mother was sitting on his bed holding his hand. Dr. Hollingsworth wasn't humming. This unemotional doctor, who had seen hundreds of people come and go, was kneeling on the floor beside the bed, praying, "Lord, I've done everything a doctor can do. Only You, the Great Physician, can save him. It's out of my hands."

Jack's stomach was horribly swollen. He was laid back on his pillow, his face gray and ashen, and he was gasping for breath.

I remember standing in line to tell him good-by. He was still unconscious. I bent over his bed and put my cheek against his and said, "Good-by, Jack." That's all I could get out.

My mother and daddy were on their knees.

At 6:30 A.M. he woke up. He opened his eyes and looked around and said, "Why is everybody crying over me? Mama, don't cry over me. Did you see the river?"

And she said, "No, I didn't, son."

"Well, I thought I was going toward the fire, but I'm headed in the other direction now, mama. I was going down a river, and there was fire on one side and heaven on the other. I was crying, 'God, I'm supposed to go to heaven. Don't You remember? Don't take me to the fire.' All of a sudden I turned, and now, mama, can you hear the angels singing?"

She said, "No, son, I can't hear it."

And he squeezed her hand and shook her arm, saying, "But mama, you've *got* to hear it." Tears started rolling off his cheeks and he said, "Mama, listen to the angels. I'm going there, mama."

We listened with astonishment.

"What a beautiful city," he said. "And the angels singing. Oh, mama, I wish you could hear the angels singing."

Those were his last words. And he died.

It was like a burden had been lifted from all of us, and it wasn't just the eight-day burden of fighting for Jack's life. Rather, we watched him die in such bliss and glory that it was like we were almost happy because of the way we saw him go. We saw in our mind's eye what he was seeing — a vision of heaven.

Jack's body was brought home to rest in our living room for Monday and Tuesday until the funeral. There were prayer meetings from time to time during the two days, and people knelt by his casket. I recall people thanking God for the influence Jack's life had brought into their lives. Somebody from over on Road Fourteen, someone we'd never seen but Jack had known, came by. Jack had delivered their papers and always had a good word for them, like, "Hope the Lord lets it rain so your cotton will grow."

At his funeral the sermon was John 14, which is preached at many funerals. Of course it has special meaning for me every time I hear it.

> *Let not your heart be troubled: ye believe in God, believe also in me. In my Father's house are many mansions: if it were not so, I would have told you. I go to prepare a place for you. And if I go and prepare a place for you, I will come again, and receive you unto myself; that where I am, there ye may be also* (1-3).

Then the songs began, like *I Am Bound for the Promised Land* and *Shall We Gather at the River*.

The memory of Jack's death, his vision of heaven, the effect his life had on the lives of others, and the image of Christ he projected have been more of an inspiration to me, I suppose, than anything else that has ever come to me through any man.

5 / **High Noon Roundup**

When we came home after the funeral, I had a great awakening in my life, a sudden new understanding. I was surprised, almost to the point of shock, to see that nothing at home had changed with Jack's death. The cottonwood trees were still green. The mockingbird was still sitting on her nest. The chickens still cackled in the chicken house. The wind was still blowing. The grass still needed cutting. The clock was still running. And Jack's Bible still lay beside the bed that he and I had shared.

I walked across the forty acres of black delta land. Didn't the world know Jack was dead? How could the cotton still dare to grow?

As I ambled alone over the little sandy rise where daddy, Jack, and I had planted watermelons, a little of the answer came to me, and it hit hard: dying is part of living.

Farther across the field was a little bayou, and right in the middle of that bayou was the tallest cypress tree for miles around. It stood all alone, just like I would learn to do now. The tree itself was dead, but the trunk still stood strong and tall. New cypress "knees" were growing up around it; little cypress trees were sprouting. At the top of the tree the limbs were broken, twisted, and gnarled by some past summer storm. Jack and I had often climbed that tree, and we had swung on the vines which clung to it.

One day the old cypress tree would fall. I would be glad. I'd never go back there. But it would be a long time falling, and the new little shoots would be a long time growing. And my grief would be a long time going.

It rained a lot that spring, and you could almost watch the crabgrass grow.

When school was out, mother, Reba, and I hoed while daddy plowed the cotton. Joanne and Tommy brought us water from the hand pump at the back door.

Mother would work in the field from about 7:00 A.M., after she finished cleaning up after breakfast, until 11:00 A.M. when she'd go in to prepare "dinner," as we called the noon meal. Then in the afternoon she'd be back in the field by 1:00 P.M. and work until 5:00, at which time she'd go in and cook supper.

Many, many times that summer of 1944, Reba and I would see tears running down mother's cheeks while she tried to keep hoeing the cotton. We'd hear her pray, "Why, Lord? Why? Why? Why?" She often said she lived only by the sustaining grace of God from one day to the next. And as the long, hot summer wore on, her grief became no less bearable.

Reba and I would sing in the cotton patch, as Jack and I had done. I'd begin early in the morning by singing one song after another while we worked. I had a knack for remembering songs I'd heard on the radio, and I'd never seem to run out of songs to sing.

In my early teen years I had a high tenor voice, and when I sang, you could hear me for miles. One of my favorite gospel groups was the Chuck Wagon Gang, and I thought the woman who sang tenor with the Gang must surely be an angel. I tried to sing like her:

> Everyday I'm camping (camping)
> In the land of Canaan (Canaan)
> And with rapture I survey
> Its wondrous beauties grand (O glory).
> Glory hallelujah,
> I have found the land of promise,
> And I'm camping,
> I'm camping,
> In Canaan's happy land.

Then I'd say, "You sing one, Reba," and she'd sing *You Are My Sunshine*.

Then I'd sing another one:

> My grandfather's clock
> Was too large for the shelf,
> So it stood ninety years on the floor;
> It was taller by half
> Than the old man himself,
> Though it weighed not
> A pennyweight more.

Then I'd say, "Your turn, Reba. Sing another one."

And she'd sing *You Are My Sunshine*.

That's the only song she knew.

And so it went. I'd sing one after the other all day long, and whenever I needed a break Reba would sing *You Are My Sunshine*.

Reba and I became fairly close the next few years. We went to the movies together on Saturday, and we walked the quarter mile back and forth to the school bus everyday. But she never took Jack's place. She never hoped to.

The whole family never missed a Sunday in church nor a Wednesday night prayer meeting. My daddy became teacher for his Sunday school class and was appointed deacon in the church.

I was getting old enough to stand around with the men outside the church before the service started and at least listen in on the conversations. There were only two subjects discussed. The prime topic was cotton.

"How's your cotton doin'?"

"Got a good stand. Hope the grass don't choke it out."

"What do you reckon it'll bring this fall, thirty-two cents?"

"Naw, when the war is over, cotton'll go down."

"I got mostly strict-middling last fall on Delta Pine seed."

"I never got more 'n fair-to-middling the whole year."

"Fair-to-middling ain't bad." (Fair-to-middling is the medium cotton grade.)

"Is this your boy, Ray?" one of the farmers would ask my daddy, talking about me.

"It sure is," said daddy.

"He's sure tall. How old is he?"

"Thirteen," said daddy. "He's gonna be a big man if he ever fills out."

As we got closer to the church service, conversation would turn to the second prime topic — the preacher. Nothing bad, nor nothing good in particular. It's just that it seemed the members of the church, and especially the men, voiced their opinions to each other each week about something the preacher had said the previous week, or something he had done during the week.

Maybe it was the church elders' way, and probably it was unintentional, of reassuring themselves that the church pastor was leading and feeding the flock properly.

The pastor of our church there at Dyess was one of those community pillars and men of God combined. A handsome, articulate man with piercing eyes and wavy black hair, he preached straight from the Bible. Hal Gallop was his name.

Rev. Gallop had announced one Sunday that he would like to take a three months' leave from the church and go away to Bible school, and that the following Sunday he'd like the church to vote on whether or not to send him. He went on to explain what a fine college he'd be going to and how much more he'd be qualified to preach and how sure he was that the congregation would agree with him that he should study those three months. He talked on and on about the benefits to all and why formal education was important to the pastor of a growing church like this one.

The following Sunday when the service began, he said with a confident smile, "Now anyone who is opposed to my going away to Bible college, please stand." The whole congregation stood.

As Rev. Gallop's smile faded and tears came to his eyes, my daddy said, "Brother Gallop, we've talked about it and have decided we can't afford to send you to Bible school. Nobody has any money in the summertime in cotton country. We are proud of you as our pastor. We believe in you because you preach the gospel. You have enough education for us."

The rest of the congregation sat down and left my daddy standing there by himself.

Rev. Gallop said, "Brother Cash, I appreciate and understand the decision of the church."

As daddy was about to take his seat, Rev. Gallop added, "Brother Cash, from time to time deacons are called upon to fulfill the pastor's duties in his absence. I

have not had a week off in three years, and next Sunday
I will be on a trip with my family. I would like you to
preach."

My daddy sat down.

Daddy never had, and still hasn't, felt the call to
preach. But every day and night of that next week in the
spring of 1945, daddy thought of nothing else except what
he would preach about.

World War II still had months to go. Everyday the
front page of the *Press-Scimitar* told us of the death and
destruction overseas.

Daddy didn't say a word to any of us about what he
would preach on, and when he walked into the pulpit that
Sunday, I was awfully proud. Everyone had been excited
that "Ray Cash is gonna preach."

Daddy was calm and confident standing there with
the Bible in his hand. He had dressed in his Sunday best,
a gray suit with a white shirt and black tie. He looked the
epitome of the southern Christian-farmer-gentleman.
His face and hands were tanned from the long hours of
work in the hot sun, and his forehead was a little lighter
shade from the hat he always wore in the fields.

After the song service he asked one of the other
deacons to "lead us in prayer." Then daddy said, "Open
up your Bibles to Second Chronicles, chapter seven, verse
fourteen," and he read aloud —

> *If my people, which are called by my name,*
> *shall humble themselves, and pray, and*
> *seek my face, and turn from their wicked*
> *ways; then will I hear from heaven, and will*
> *forgive their sin, and will heal their land.*

For thirty minutes I listened enthralled while
daddy gave a timeless message on a nation's woes and
grief which come from not obeying God, a message that

would apply to the world condition today just as much as it did in 1945.

The congregation surrounded him at the front afterwards, handshaking and complimenting him. I'm sure my grandfather, Rev. William Henry Cash, would have been proud, too.

When we worked in the fields in the summertime, we usually took an hour off for lunch from noon till 1:00. We ate at 12:00, then from 12:30 to 1:00 we listened to the "High Noon Roundup" over WMPS, Memphis, featuring Smilin' Eddie Hill and Ira and Charlie Louvin, the Louvin Brothers. It was a half-hour variety show of songs, talk, and lots of country comedy which was just what we needed to get us over the "hump" of a long day in the fields. Smilin' Eddie Hill hosted the program before a live studio audience, and he was quite a character. People all over the Mid-South listened to and talked about the show.

I usually managed to stretch my lunch hour to 1:15 because at 1:00, for fifteen minutes, Eddie Hill and the Louvin Brothers, calling themselves the Lonesome Valley Trio, sang gospel songs. This had to be my all-time favorite radio program. I loved the way Eddie Hill changed his personality, and even his voice, when he finished "High Noon Roundup" and went into the gospel program.

"Howdy friends and neighbors. This is Eddie Hill with Ira and Charlie, the Louvin Brothers. We've got fifteen minutes of good ol' gospel for you. Thank you for your requests. We want to do our first song today for Jim Warren of Wilson, Arkansas, who asks that it be sent out to his mother, Mrs. Sadie Warren, of Lepanto, Arkansas, who is sick and shut-in. The Lord bless you, Mrs. Warren. Here's your song."

We read of a place that's called heaven,
It's made for the pure and the free;

> These truths in God's Word He hath given,
> How beautiful heaven must be.
>
> How beautiful heaven must be (must be),
> Sweet home of the happy and free;
> Fair haven of rest for the weary,
> How beautiful heaven must be.

One day in the spring of 1947, Eddie Hill announced that the entire "High Noon Roundup" would make a personal appearance at the Dyess High School auditorium. And for the next couple of weeks that was all I thought about and all I talked about — seeing Eddie and Ira and Charlie in person!

The night of the show I was at the school two hours early to watch them drive up and unload their equipment. I'd never seen such a big car. I suppose it was a limousine, though I'd never heard of one at that time. A mountain of musical instruments, a sound system, and souvenir books and pictures were unloaded by the seven or eight people who were in the car.

I recognized the Louvin Brothers from pictures I'd seen of them in the paper.

Ira headed for the auditorium carrying his mandolin as carefully as a baby, but Charlie Louvin walked right over to me, and I could see that he was about to speak to me. A lump came up in my throat. I'd never been that close to a radio star. I had so many things I wanted to tell him about how I loved the show, the hymn program. I wanted to tell him I could sing just like Ira with my high voice. I wanted to tell him, "I'm going to be a singer on the radio someday, too."

Charlie said, "Hi, where's the rest room?"

"I'll show you," I said, and I led him down the sidewalk to the boys' rest room. That lump in my throat wouldn't go away.

When he came out, I walked beside him back to the auditorium. He reached in his pocket and pulled out a couple of soda crackers and started eating them. With all the things I'd wanted to talk to Charlie about, I couldn't say a word. But here I was actually walking beside one of those voices I'd loved so much.

"Are those crackers good for your throat?" I finally asked.

"Good for your belly if you're hungry," said Charlie, and he disappeared into the auditorium. (For years afterwards I ate soda crackers every time I could get my hands on them.)

The show was everything I'd hoped it would be. Eddie Hill was really "on" with his jokes and shenanigans. Ira Louvin did a takeoff on a woman character he called Sal Skinner and brought the house down. All their radio musicians were there: "Lightning" Chance, Paul Buskirke, Tony Cinciola, the whole crew. I sat up front row center and told all my friends I had talked to Charlie Louvin and that I knew why he could sing like that (soda crackers)!

After a few more hymns and gospel songs by the Lonesome Valley Trio, the show was over, and I watched them pack the instruments in the car.

There were a few people around them getting autographs and talking to them, but I knew I couldn't say a word. Nobody would believe what I wanted to say anyway: "I'll be up there someday. That's what I'm gonna be." I had no doubt.

I waved to them as they pulled out and took off in a cloud of dust down Road One toward the Memphis highway. Charlie waved back, and how much that meant to me. It was like it had been when I was three years old standing by the railroad track and waving at the engineer as the train went by. It was awfully important that the engineer waved back. I'd shout, "He saw me! He waved!"

That's the way I felt when Charlie Louvin waved

at me. "He remembered me," I thought. "He knows I'm the one who showed him the rest room — the one that's going to be a singer."

But then Charlie Louvin couldn't really help but notice me. I was the only one left at the auditorium standing under that single light outside the stage door. I watched the taillights on that limousine disappear down the dirt road, and then I started home.

I didn't even feel the gravel on my bare feet that night when I walked the two-and-a-half miles home in the dark, singing all the songs I'd heard from the stage at the school auditorium.

I felt an eager anticipation about my future, an exciting expectation of the years coming in which I knew I'd be on that stage singing those songs I loved. Not only those precious old ones, but new ones as yet unwritten.

In school I spent a lot of time daydreaming, and soon began putting those daydreams down on paper. Besides writing short stories and poems, I drew pictures of tall buildings in cities I'd never seen.

They asked me to sing at school assemblies — songs like *Trees* and *Wiffenpoof Song* and *Drink to Me Only With Thine Eyes* — which I did, though they really weren't songs I wanted to sing.

I had no accompaniment and no microphone, but I didn't need a mike. Nobody had any trouble hearing my strong, high voice. It was the country songs, or the "hillbilly" songs as we called them then, that I wanted to do.

"Let me do a gospel song," I would ask my teacher. But even in Dyess, Arkansas, at a very proper and official high school assembly, *Whiffenpoof Song*, I was told, would be more appropriate.

"Or what about a poem?" I suggested.

"What poem?" the teacher asked.

"One I wrote," I said.
"Let's hear it."

When I consider
Why that I
Was made to live
And made to die,
And know no more
Than what I'm told
In what the Book says,
Centuries old;

My mind goes flying
Far away
To those six great
Creation days,
When light first shone
And trees first grew
When waters ran
And eagles flew;

Then He saw fit
To make me last
To live a life —
And then it's past. . .

There must have been a reason!

"It's too short," she said. "Sing the
Whiffenpoof Song."
I didn't play football or basketball on the Dyess
team; there was always work to do in the fields after
school. In the spring we plowed and hoed. In the fall and
winter we picked the cotton.
Then, there was Virginia North — I had a crush
on her and had long been thinking that if we had a car
and if there was some place to take her, I'd ask
her to go with me. She had dated a boy from Osceola,
Arkansas, the county seat. And that was supposed
to be a really big deal when a Dyess girl went with some-

one from Osceola, or better still Blytheville, an even
bigger town. I had seen her with him driving through
Dyess one Saturday afternoon, and it was a painful sight
for me.

Virginia was always friendly at school; she smiled
and talked with me a lot, which only made me fall
harder for her. I wrote her love letters that I never gave her.
The whole year went by, and I thought I'd surely die if
I couldn't take Virginia North to the movies, or something.

At last, in the winter of 1947 we got our first car,
a 1935 Ford with mechanical brakes. Usually the brakes
didn't work at all, but when they did work, they
worked *too* good.

The car, though, was a godsend — especially
to mother and daddy. A car of our own to drive to church
meant we wouldn't have to beg a ride with Ted Fox,
our neighbor across the road. We had always ridden in the
back of Ted Fox's pickup truck to and from church,
two-and-a-half miles in summer and winter.

It wasn't long before all the windows were broken
out in the old Ford. They were literally shaken to pieces
by the bumps on the rough gravel road. When it was
raining or very cold, we put slats of cardboard in where the
windows had been. And there was no heater. But it was
still better protection than the bed of Ted Fox's pickup.

One rainy Saturday afternoon, about the time I
turned sixteen, I drove up to the Dyess Cafe, the weekend
gathering place for the town's teenagers. Nobody ever
ate a complete meal there, just a hot dog or a hamburger
when affordable or maybe only a nickel in the jukebox to
hear Eddy Arnold or Red Foley.

Dyess had a town circle instead of a town square,
so I wheeled quickly around the circle throwing up all kinds
of gravel and then whipped around to park at the Cafe.
And there, standing on the porch, was Virginia North.
I slammed on the brakes. But there were no brakes. So I spun

the steering wheel around and slid into the porch of the
cafe sideways. Virginia jumped back to avoid getting hit just
in time to watch all the cardboard windows pop out
from the impact and drop to the ground.

She stood there smiling at me. And I, in at least
my second year of being madly in love with her, took her
smile as a kind of invitation.

"How about a date tonight?" I said as I stepped
up on the porch out of the rain — with all the boldness
and confidence I would have had if I'd been captain of
the basketball team.

Her smile quickly faded. She took a step
backwards, looked at the car, looked back at me and said,
"I might go with you sometime if you had *windows* in
your car."

She turned around and went inside the cafe,
leaving me standing there.

I jumped in the car, started the engine, and
splattered mud and gravel all over the front of the cafe
as I sped for home.

With the cold, wet rain blowing in my face,
I wanted to cry for awhile. Instead, I decided to laugh.

"So long, Virginia North," I said to myself.
"I'll have a car with windows in it someday — and you'll
be stuck picking cotton somewhere up around Osceola!"

I started singing. All the way home I sang the
song that had been playing on the jukebox at the cafe.
It was George Morgan's *Candy Kisses,* and it was kind
of appropriate.

> Candy kisses wrapped in paper
> Mean more to you than any of mine.
> Candy kisses wrapped in paper
> You'd rather have them any old time.
>
> By George Morgan, © 1948 Hill and Range Songs, Inc. Used by permission.

In the spring of 1948, my mother got excited about
my singing. She had me sing several "specials" at the

church, but the keys she played in on the piano were either too low or too high for me, so I didn't enjoy it; and I don't think anyone else did except my mother. But she encouraged me to keep singing.

Her father, John L. Rivers, had "led the singing" at the little Crossroads Methodist Church near Kingsland, Arkansas, for forty years. I think she saw her father in me from time to time. She often told me I looked like him, that I was going to be tall like he was.

But she couldn't understand my high tenor voice. "My daddy had a low, booming voice," she'd say.

"My voice will change," I thought.

Then I was scared. "What if I can't sing after it changes?"

I worried about that a lot.

One day later in the summer my dad and I cut wood from dawn to dusk. I swung the ax and pulled the crosscut saw with him for six hours. We sat under a tree at noon and ate a big lunch of biscuits, ham, sausage, eggs, and milk my mother had packed for us. Then we cut wood for six more hours.

When I came in the back door of the kitchen where my mother was cooking supper that evening, I was unconsciously singing to myself.

She wheeled around and said in surprise, "Who was that singing in such a low, booming voice?"

"That was me," I said, almost as surprised as she.

"Sing some more," said mama.

> Everybody's gonna have religion in glory.
> Everybody's gonna be singing the story.
> Everybody's gonna have a wonderful time up
>   there,
> O glory hallelujah.
> Brother, there's a reckonin' comin' in the
>   morning.
> Better get you ready,

'Cause I'm giving you the warning.
Everybody's gonna have a wonderful time up
there.

My mother's eyes were full of tears. "You sound exactly like my daddy," she said.

"Hey! Did you hear that?" I was excited. "My voice dropped! Listen how low I can go! Boom Ba Ba Boom Ba Ba, Boom Ba Ba Boom Ba Ba." I *could* sing low.

"God has His hand on you, son," said mama.

She stood back and looked at me. "I don't know exactly what He has in mind, but God has His hand on you."

As we sat down to supper that night, to a table covered with good hot food for two hungry woodcutters, nothing else was said about it. But for some reason, I felt my mother was right.

6 / **Ragged Old Flag**

In July of 1950, I entered the U. S. Air Force. The first year I was in the states at three different bases. After radio operating school, they sent me to Germany in the Security Service as a radio intercept operator.

My daddy was proud of me for enlisting. As I said earlier, he was a World War I veteran, and service in America's military had been a duty the Cash men performed for three hundred years. Maybe that's one reason why I love my country so much and believe in it so strongly. A lot of family blood has been shed for it. It's that American heritage which compelled me to write *Ragged Old Flag*.

> I walked through a county courthouse square,
> On a park bench an old man was sitting there.
> I said, "Your old courthouse is kinda run down."
> He said, "Naw, it'll do for our little town."
> I said, "Your old flagpole has leaned a little bit,
> And that's a *Ragged Old Flag* you got hanging on it."
>
> He said, "Have a seat," and I sat down.

"Is this the first time you've been to our little
    town?"
I said, "I think it is." He said, "I don't like to
    brag,
But we're kinda proud of that *Ragged Old
    Flag.*

"You see, we got a little hole in that flag there
When Washington took it across the
    Delaware.
And it got powder-burned the night Francis
    Scott Key
Sat watching it writing *Say Can You See.*
And it got a bad rip in New Orleans
With Packingham and Jackson tuggin' at its
    seams.

"And it almost fell at the Alamo
Beside the Texas flag, but she waved on
    though.
She got cut with a sword at Chancellorsville
And she got cut again at Shiloh Hill.
There was Robert E. Lee, Beauregard, and
    Bragg,
And the south wind blew hard on that
    Ragged Old Flag.

"On Flanders Field in World War I
She got a big hole from a Bertha gun.
She turned blood red in World War II.
She hung limp and low by the time it was
    through.
She was in Korea and Vietnam.
She went where she was sent by her Uncle
    Sam.

"She waved from our ships upon the briny
    foam,
And now they've about quit waving her back
    here at home.
In her own good land here she's been
    abused —

She's been burned, dishonored, denied, and
  refused.

"And the government for which she stands
Is scandalized throughout the land.
And she's getting threadbare and wearing
  thin,
But she's in good shape for the shape she's in.
'Cause she's been through the fire before
And I believe she can take a whole lot more.

"So we raise her up every morning, take her
  down every night.
We don't let her touch the ground and we fold
  her up right.
On second thought I do like to brag,
'Cause I'm mighty proud of that *Ragged Old
  Flag*."

By John R. Cash, © 1974 House of Cash, Inc.

When I enlisted, a lot of guys in the service had a
set policy — when they got their three-day passes they'd
stay drunk three days, come back and work six days, then
hit another three-day drunk. I didn't drink, and there
were a few other guys in my outfit who didn't drink, so I
chose to run with them. Usually the thing I would find in
common with friends was that we shared a love for music.
Boys from my part of the country — four or five of them
— played guitar and mandolin and banjo in the service.

We were pretty rough and raw musically, but I
don't think I ever enjoyed pickin' any more than I did
during those cold nights in Germany, singing songs like *The
Wild Side of Life, Movin' On, Dim Lights, Thick
Smoke*, and the *Great Speckled Bird*. Invariably when we
had a session, we'd always come back to the gospel
songs. We'd sing three or four-part harmony before the
night was over, and those songs had a way of taking us
back home.

Practically everybody in Germany drank beer,

and when *everybody* does it, then, as with many other things, we make the mistake of telling ourselves it's all right.

As the long weeks and months went by, Dyess, Arkansas, and that little church, and the things I'd learned there, and the life I'd lived there became more and more distant. The letters to my loved ones at home slowed up, then stopped.

From beer I graduated to German Cognac and having more wild times. And I guess I started to be a fairly profane person because for the first time in my life I got to seeing how good I could curse. The booze and the profanity began launching me into all kinds of other habits which soon became second nature.

I worshiped at the base chapel fairly regularly for the first year or so, but working shift work, sometimes midnight to eight, eight to five, or five to midnight, I often made believe I had a good excuse for not attending church. Finally I stopped going altogether, as my drinking habit increased. The third year I was in Germany, having broken away from church, I joined the boozers on each three-day pass. Though occasionally I'd spend a three-day pass fishing with Bill Carnahan and Ted Freeman, two of my best friends.

One of our favorite fishing spots was a trout stream at a town named GrossKitscherkoffen. We caught fish, drank our beer, and cooked the fish in the middle of the town square. We always ended up in trouble with the local police for disturbing the peace, but they usually ran us out of town rather than lock us up.

Another favorite fishing spot ran through the Bavarian village of Oberammergau. Oberammergau is famous worldwide for the passion play held every ten years reenacting the crucifixion of Jesus Christ.

We had several good fishing spots, but the stream at Oberammergau was the best one. And we seemed to drink less beer at Oberammergau than we did at the other places.

The mountains around the village were breath-takingly beautiful, and sitting on our case of beer as the day wore on, we'd talk about the passion play. Then, of course, we'd start talking about Jesus and God and religion like a Christian can't seem to keep from doing when he's drinking too much.

Those days at Oberammergau always ended on a more sober, peaceful note, and I'd return to the base with a little gnawing at my conscience. Not from the beer, especially, but because the spirit of the environment at Oberammergau reminded me of the church and my people back home and of the Master I had once walked closely with, but now only occasionally spoke to.

I took a part in most everything else that goes along with drunkenness that last year in Germany each time the three-day passes came around, which actually wasn't very often. Between passes I worked hard at my job in Air Force Security Service.

I returned to the United States as a Staff Sergeant and was honorably discharged July 4, 1954. I had a crooked nose from a fight with a paratrooper in a honky-tonk, a scar on my cheek left by a drunken German doctor who couldn't find a cyst he was trying to remove, and a left ear with the hearing temporarily impaired because a German girl stuck a pencil in it. Otherwise, I was in good shape to come back home to my people and to a San Antonio girl named Vivian Liberto, whom I married a month later.

Vivian and I had corresponded during the three years I'd been in Germany. She was Catholic and came from devout Catholic parents. Some of her people and some of mine were deeply concerned about our difference in religion. Our reply was the same one given by countless young couples in like circumstances: "We worship the same God." "There's just one Jesus." But we knew it really was a problem worth careful consideration.

I agreed that any children born of the marriage would be reared according to her Catholic direction and that I would ensure and agree that they attend the Catholic church, be instructed in catechism, and observe all rules and ordinances of the Catholic church. We were married by her uncle, Father Vincent Liberto, from New Orleans.

After our marriage, my spiritual path took some strange avenues. I took a six-month instruction course in Catholicism with a priest in Memphis at the suggestion of Vivian's father, Tom Liberto, one of the finest Christians I've ever known. I drove Vivian to Catholic services at 9:00 A.M., then went alone to my Protestant service at 10:30.

The Catholic instruction gave me an understanding and a tolerance for other faiths which I value today. In all the years Vivian and I were married, one thing we never argued about, nor had a cross word about, was religion. I understood her beliefs, her church doctrine. I never questioned her faith, for I knew it was real. And I knew the Catholic church service provided her a way to truly worship.

When our beautiful little daughters, Rosanne, Kathleen, Cindy, and Tara, came along, I usually took them to church when I was home. Though I never personally instructed them in Catholicism, I encouraged it at home. I knew how some of my people felt about this, so I always tried to avoid the subject in discussion with them. From time to time I let my daughters know and understand my beliefs, and I'd explain salvation as I knew it. But I lived up to my marriage vows that they be reared Catholic.

We had real love and peace in our home for a long

time. The old habits I'd acquired in Germany were
ended. I never had really liked alcohol, so it was easy for
me to abstain. But more than that, I was beginning my
marriage with determination to make it work.

I got a job as a salesman with an appliance and hom
improvement company in Memphis, a job for which I
was completely ill-suited. But with a baby on the way, car
payments to make, and rent to pay on our little
apartment, I knocked on doors all day long, trying as best I
knew how to sell refrigerators, washing machines,
aluminum siding, and ornamental iron.

One day, after an especially long series of having
doors slammed in my face, I knocked on the last door for
the afternoon. When the lady of the house answered my
knock, I said, "You don't want to buy anything either,
do you, ma'am?"

"I don't know. What are you selling?"

"Nothing," I said.

"Then why did you knock on my door?" she
asked.

"So you could make my day complete by telling
me no," I said.

"You better get away from my door before I call
the police," she sputtered.

"How about a used washing machine? It's only
had nine previous owners," I said, chuckling as she
slammed the door in my face.

I couldn't really get my mind on anything but
music. I spent more time in my car listening to the radio
than I did knocking on doors.

At night I'd lay awake for hours listening to the
record shows. There were a couple of songs I had written
in Germany that I sang for my friends and family. Their
encouragement and approval only increased my
burning desire to be a part of the music world.

In what I called my "little black book," I had written down the names and addresses of everyone I knew. Thumbing through its pages one morning early, I saw a name: John Bell, Radio Station WMCA, Corinth, Miss.

The name had been given me by Tom Weaver, an Air Force friend in Germany. Tom had told me, "If you want to break into radio as an announcer or disc jockey, go see John Bell in Corinth. He might be able to help you."

I turned my green '54 Plymouth southeast toward Corinth, and a couple of hours later walked into the WMCA studio offices. There was John Bell's name on a door, and I started to walk in, but I heard someone singing down the hall from behind the plate glass window of the control room.

The singer was Buddy Bain. He was finishing up his program, telling where he was going to be on personal appearances. I waited until he came out.

"I heard you on the radio driving down from Memphis," I said. "Your singing sounded good."

"Glad to meet you," he said as he continued toward the front door.

"Do you think I could see Mr. Bell?" I asked.

"Maybe so," he said. "What about?"

"About a job," I said. "I'm a singer — and also an announcer." I laid it on a little too thick, too quick, so I added, "Do you know Tom Weaver? He's a friend of mine."

"I sure do," said Buddy. "Is he still in Germany?"

"I think so," I said.

He opened John Bell's door and stuck his head in. "Can you see a friend of Tom Weaver?" Buddy asked.

John Bell was very kind to me.

"So you're going to be in radio," he said. "What makes you think so?"

"I don't *think* so," I said. "I *know* so. I'm going to be a singer making records someday. But until I can do that, I could be a good announcer or disc jockey if you'd give me a chance."

"What makes you think you can handle the job? Have you had any experience?" he asked.

"No sir," I said.

"Have you ever so much as spoken into a microphone?" he asked.

"No sir," I admitted.

"Sorry, I don't have a job for you," he said. "As a matter of fact, I don't think you're going to get one on guts alone. You need a little training."

"Where can I get the training?" I asked.

"Try Keegan's School of Broadcasting in Memphis," he said. "You can go there on the GI Bill. Then come see me when you've finished the course."

"Will you give me a job then?" I pursued.

"I'm not sure," he smiled. "But you'll be qualified to talk about it."

I enrolled in Keegan's school, training to be a staff announcer, news broadcaster, and disc jockey, going only part-time because I still had to try to make a living. I continued in the school for five months, enjoying every minute of it — especially the hours when I "played" disc jockey. I prayed for an open door to find my way into the music world.

And I began to see a way, although many doors would be difficult to open.

My brother Roy introduced me to two mechanic friends, Marshall Grant who played bass and Luther Perkins who played electric guitar. We three became friends and "made music" together practically every night at Roy's house or at mine. Friends and neighbors started coming in and listening, and we'd sing and play until the early hours of the morning, night after night, just for the love of it.

I sang all the country songs that were popular, all the old ones that suited my voice, and Marshall would join in singing tenor on the gospel songs. He knew them all.

He was from the mountains of North Carolina, and he'd learned them from the radio as I had.

Luther Perkins, with his unique "boom-chicka-boom" on the guitar, was the son of a Baptist preacher from Mississippi. So it was only natural that he was at home with those songs.

It was fitting that our first public appearance was a performance in a church in North Memphis. One of our neighbors who had heard us asked if we'd do a few songs in their Sunday night service.

We had talked about clothes and thought we should try to dress alike, but nobody had a nice suit, and the only colored shirts we had alike were black.

"Black will be better for church anyway," I said, so we wore black shirts and pants.

(To this day, when someone asks me why I wear black, I can never really think of a simple answer, so I often say, "Black is better for church.")

We walked down the side aisle of the sanctuary, and Luther set his little worn-out amplifier on the pulpit. Marshall set down his big bass fiddle, taped and glued together, and I had my five-dollar guitar that I'd brought home from Germany.

I sang three or four gospel songs, then introduced one I had written myself called *Belshazzar*.

> The people feasted and drank their wine,
> And praised the false gods of the time.
> All holy things they scorned and mocked,
> But suddenly all their mocking stopped,
> For on the wall there appeared a hand,
> Nothing else — there was no man.
> In blood the hand began to write,
> And Belshazzar couldn't hide his fright.
>
> He was weighed in the balance
> And found wanting;
> His kingdom was divided, couldn't stand.

> He was weighed in the balance
> And found wanting;
> His houses were built upon the sand.

The response to my songs that night made me feel a door had opened. Were some of my prayers getting through?

The big door I had my eye on was Sun Record Company, where Elvis Presley had recently started. When I finally got Sam Phillips, the owner of Sun, on the phone, he was very kind, but very firm in his rejection.

I told him about *Belshazzar* and asked for an audition.

"I love those hymns and gospel songs, too, John, but we have to sell records to stay in business. We're a small company and can't afford to speculate on a new artist singing gospel."

"I'm going to record them, Mr. Phillips. I don't know when, but I know I'm going to," I said.

"Well, good luck to you." And he hung up.

"Why didn't I tell him I've got other songs? He might like *Folsom Prison Blues*," I said to myself later.

Next time I went in person, but I couldn't get in without an appointment. So I called him again. An audition was refused. I waited a week and called again.

"You don't give up, do you, John?" said Sam Phillips.

"No, sir," I answered.

"Come on down and let's hear what you've got."

Marshall and Luther met me at Sun Records, and I sang all day — Hank Snow songs, Jimmie Rodgers, Ernest Tubb, the old ones, the new ones, and finally my own.

Though he had discouraged it earlier, the first one of my songs I sang was *Belshazzar,* and Sam recorded it

on tape. Then I sang other songs of mine, *Hey Porter* and
Folsom Prison Blues.

"I'll give you a contract," said Sam. "But you'll
have to leave it to me to decide what is more commercial.
I have to release what I believe is right for the market."

"That's fine with me," I said.

Two of my songs, the railroad ballad called *Hey
Porter* and a weeper called *Cry, Cry, Cry,* were released
first. I ran over to radio station WMPS with my first copy of
the big 78 rpm record. Bob Neal was the disc jockey
who put it on the turntable, and he smiled his approval as
Hey Porter began to play. The yellow Sun label went
around and around, and I breathed a prayer of thanks for
this dream come true. He turned the record over and
played the other side, then played side one again.

The "big door" was beginning to open for me.

That night I went home and wrote a song which
concerned "tithing" my music and called it *My Prayer.* It
was recorded three years later on Columbia records in my
first hymn album and renamed *Lead Me, Father.* It was
never a big seller, but every few days for the last twenty
years I have sung this song over in my mind, if not
aloud:

> When my hands get tired,
> When my steps get slow,
> Walk beside me and give me the strength to
>   go.
> Fill my face with Your courage,
> So defeat won't show,
> And pick me up when I stumble,
> So the world won't know.
>
> Lead me, Father, with the staff of life,
> And give me the strength for a song.
> That the words I sing
> Might more strength bring,

To help some poor troubled weary worker
along.

When my way is clear,
And I fail to see,
With Thy strong hands
Strike out the blindness in me.
Show me work that I should
Carry on for Thee.
Make my way straight and narrow
As You would have it be.

7 / I Walk the Line

My first public appearance after the record was released came in the form of a guest appearance with singer Sonny James at a Saturday night country show in the armory at Covington, Tennessee.

I was well aware of the fact that the private lives of entertainers are anything but private. The public knows or will soon know the moral and spiritual position of any entertainer who comes on the scene. They know which ones are straight and which are not. There is no better light by which to read what is really on a person's face than a spotlight. From the beginning I realized the importance of staying straight and walking with God, not only for myself, but as an influence on others.

Sonny James had been in show business all his life, and I knew him to be a truly committed Christian. I had to talk to him about it for I sensed the pitfalls and temptations I would face.

I had gone on stage earlier with Marshall and Luther and had done my two songs. The audience kept calling me back, and I did both of them three or four times. From that first appearance, I felt complete acceptance by the crowd. Somehow I knew I was on my way.

When my part of the show was over, I wanted to stay out of the noise and confusion in the dressing room, so I found myself a place to peep through the curtain backstage and watch Sonny James. He was an excellent entertainer. He sang ballads, novelty songs, and his hits. He did a comedy routine — played the fiddle upside down, backwards, with his feet, standing on his head. Then he closed with a hymn, *The Last Leaf:*

> My life is in Thy hands, oh Lord;
> I give it all to Thee.
> And until death I'll carry on
> Till the last leaf shall fall from the tree.
>
> By Bodie Chandler-Edward McKendry,
> © 1963 Warner-Tamerlane Publishing Corp. All rights reserved.
> Used by permission of Warner Bros. Music.

When he came off, I waited around for a few minutes and then cornered him. "Sonny," I said, "I know you're a Christian, and so am I. I know I was meant to be in the music and entertainment world, but how do you live a Christian life in this business?"

Sonny thought for a minute. "John," he said, "the way I do it is by *being* what I am. I am not just an entertainer who became a Christian. I am a Christian who chose to be an entertainer. I am first a Christian."

"But what about the songs?" I asked. "It looks like my first record is doing OK, and the people seem to like it, but I'm not sure it's the kind of song I want to record."

"The people will decide that for you, John. Have you got anything else recorded?"

"Yes," I said. "A song I wrote called *Folsom Prison Blues*. Sam Phillips thinks it's going to be a big one."

"Sam probably knows," said Sonny.

"I enjoy performing, and to enjoy it you have to know your audience enjoys it," I said. "But I want to be able to sing everything I like as well, including the hymns."

Sonny said, "If tonight is any indication of how successful you're going to be, I'd say you've got it made. Don't worry. Sooner or later you'll be singing everything you want to. You've got to build your following first. Give them what they want to hear."

"I will," I said, "but I just feel like I'm not giving my best."

Sonny said, "Remember that what you are and the life you live sings louder than any song."

"Thanks for the advice," I said. "I really appreciate it."

"Don't forget to pray," Sonny said.

In the summer of 1955 I performed my first major concert appearance as guest on Elvis Presley's show at Overton Park Shell in Memphis.

At the bottom of the ad in the Memphis *Press-Scimitar* promoting Elvis's show, in very small print it read, "Extra — Johnny Cash sings *Cry, Cry, Cry*." Actually, I did two songs on the show, *Cry, Cry, Cry* and *Hey Porter,* and I was satisfied with the appearance.

All my family, friends, and everyone who knew me were there to see me officially launch my career. The audience called me back, and I did the newly recorded but as yet unreleased *Folsom Prison Blues.*

Then I stood backstage and watched Elvis. I had seen him at his first couple of appearances. One was at the grand opening of the Katz Drug Store in South Memphis, the other was at a ballroom in East Memphis. The audience reaction to him was always the same. The girls and women screamed, cried, and fainted, and though the men might be jealous, nobody could keep from watching him. He had, and has, a personal magnetism on and offstage — but especially onstage — that is unique.

I met Carl Perkins at Sun Records studios one day in that summer of '55. He was there recording his second

session with his brothers, Jay and Clayton, and drummer
W. S. Holland.

"Is Johnny Cash your real name?" Carl asked.

"Yes, it is. At least Cash is. Sam put Johnny on the
record, but John is good enough."

"Glad to meet you, John," said Carl.

"Same here," I said. "I like your record *Movie
Mag*."

"I loved that *Cry, Cry, Cry,* too," said Carl.
"Let's do some shows together some time."

"OK, let's do."

And so began one of the longest, truest friendships
of my life — a friendship that has spanned over twenty
years and has stood the test of good times and bad.

We have a lot in common, Carl and I. He was
raised in the flat black land in West Tennessee just across
the river from my Arkansas home, and though he found his
place in the music world through rock and roll, his heart
is really in country and gospel music which he performs
superbly.

There have been times Carl has been closer than a
brother, and I've often seen my brother Jack in Carl. He
and I are the same age, yet in times of great depression, Carl
often counseled me and befriended me with a wisdom
beyond his years.

And the befriending worked both ways.

That day in '55 I said, "I've got another booking
with Elvis in Amory, Mississippi, two weeks from
Friday night."

"I'm on that show, too," said Carl.

"How about the following week?" I asked. "I'm
guesting on the "Louisiana Hayride" in Shreveport,
Louisiana, and then I'm booked in Gladewater, Texas.
How about being on those shows with me?"

"We'll be there," Carl said.

Elvis Presley walked into the studio and sat down

at the piano and played and sang *Blueberry Hill.* Then,
he did a blues-type gospel song.

I had heard the same gospel "feeling" in some of
his records and wasn't surprised at all when he said,
"Let's sing some gospel." We started humming, finding
our places in the songs Elvis was playing.

Sam Phillips walked over and said, "I hate to
interrupt, but before you do another song, I'd like for
you boys to meet a fantastic talent I've just auditioned. I
plan to record him." We all shook hands with Jerry Lee
Lewis.

"And this is Jack Clement," said Sam,
introducing us to the boy who had been standing in the
control room with him. "Jack is going to help me engineer
and produce some of your sessions."

I had no idea what "engineer and produce"
meant, so I said, "That's fine." It wasn't until several
months later when I went in to record and Jack Clement
was the only one there that I realized what Sam meant.
Jack Clement was going to be in charge of recording me —
"my producer" I guess you'd say. And "produce" he did.

I would work well with Jack Clement, recording
*Guess Things Happen That Way, Ballad of a Teenage
Queen,* and many others. Later, Jack would introduce
me to Charlie Rich, and I'd record some of his songs, like
Ways of a Woman in Love.

"Do you know *Will the Circle Be Unbroken?"*
Jerry asked Elvis.

"Yeah," Elvis said as he began playing the
melody.

"Do you guys mind if I turn on the recorder?"
Jack Clement asked.

"Go ahead," we answered.

> Will the circle be unbroken
> By and by, Lord, by and by?

> In a better home awaiting
> In the sky, Lord, in the sky?

The four of us, Elvis, Carl, Jerry Lee, and I, sang eight or ten old hymn favorites. After awhile Elvis stood up and Jerry Lee sat down at the piano. He played it like I'd never heard before, and we all stood and watched him.

He played and sang a song which brought back memories from three or four years earlier — *There Are Strange Things Happening Every Day* — and nobody could do it like Jerry Lee.

> More and more along the way
> I hear church people say,
> There are strange things happening every day.
> Every day, yes, every day.
> There are strange things happening every day.

I thought back to a friend of mine from the Air Force, C. V. White, who'd had an album by black singer Sister Rosetta Tharpe. And that song was on the album. C. V. would let me borrow that record album about once a week, and I'd listen to her sing that song over and over again.

When we heard Jerry Lee Lewis do *Strange Things,* we knew Sam *had* found a great talent.

I have never heard the tape from that impromptu session that day. But I have been told that a tape exists, locked away in a bank vault in Memphis, of a rough, unrehearsed quartet of would-be singers who, with no commercial reasons in mind, gathered around the piano back in the summer of '55 and put their hearts into eight or ten good songs.

That day was the beginning of a long friendship, not only with Carl Perkins, but with the others I met and would meet around Sun Records. As time went by we all worked many shows together — Elvis, Carl, Jerry Lee, and I, though Elvis soon changed to another record company, then later went into the army, and we didn't see him much after that.

Another long-time and true friend I was to meet at Sun was Roy Orbison, who became one of the all-time greatest record sellers internationally. I worked many tours with Roy, and he is a kind, sensitive person who puts his whole heart into writing and performing.

The memories of those early beginnings at Sun Records and that spirited talent I was privileged to work with are precious to me; we all got along so well. I cannot recall any show of jealousy on the part of anyone. We constantly were helping each other, supporting each other during concerts, and we all shared together in those early successes.

Backstage in Amory, Mississippi, on the Friday night two weeks later, I sat talking with Carl Perkins. He and I had already performed, and Elvis was onstage.

"I thought they were going to tear your clothes off out there tonight, Carl. I believe you encored about nine times, didn't you?" I said.

"I've been here before, and they're always good to me, John," Carl said.

"I watched you tonight," I said, "and you really have a feel for the 'bop' kind of song. Why don't you record one?"

"I've sung that kind of music all my life, John, the rhythm and blues and gospel songs with the beat, but I haven't come up with the right song yet."

"Carl," I said, "when I was in the Air Force, there was this black staff sergeant from Virginia named C. V. White who was the live wire in the organization. He was funny; he always had a laugh and smile for everybody. He'd dress up as sharp as a tack with his uniform pressed, his cap cocked on the side of his head, and he'd come into my room saying, 'How do I look, man?'

"I'd say, 'Mighty spiffy, C. V.'

"He'd say, 'Just don't step on my blue suede shoes, man,' and he'd trip out the door snapping his fingers.

" 'Hey, C. V.!' I'd yell. 'Those are Air Force regulation shoes, not blue suede.'

" 'Tonight when I get to town they're gonna be blue suede, man,' C. V. would yell back at me with a smile.''

"That's a great idea for a bop song!" Carl said.

"That's why I told you," I said. "With the feel you have for that kind of music, you're the man who should write it."

Carl grabbed a pencil and a piece of brown paper sack and started writing. Before Elvis came offstage, he had written *Blue Suede Shoes*.

"I'll sing it for you in Gladewater Sunday night," Carl said as I left Amory for home.

Early the next morning I said good-by and left for Shreveport and Gladewater. Even then I think Vivian realized a lot better than I did that my trips away from home, the tours, my complete involvement in the music business would be the beginning of the end of our marriage.

We had a baby and another one on the way. Vivian was concerned with making a home, and once she saw the music world was going to separate us, she showed little interest in it.

Year after year, as my career took me away for more and more concert tours, as more demands were placed upon my time, she fought against the rat race in every way she could. The more the world pulled me away, the harder she pulled in the other direction, trying to hold me in a family bond.

She would only give up and divorce me in order to save herself and the girls after my drug habit robbed me not only of my will to be a husband and father, but also voided my conscience which could no longer govern my judgment. But I didn't know it was the beginning of the end for us. I was concerned only with living my "dream come true."

The reaction of the audience that night at the "Louisiana Hayride" in Shreveport was intoxicating. People came from all over the South and Southwest to the Hayride which was broadcast live over radio station KWKH.

It was on this tour — two weeks after my record had come out — that I was twisting the radio dial and heard *Hey Porter* playing. When the announcer gave the call letters KWKH, I ran to a phone and called Sam Phillips. I was so excited I was bursting with joy.

"I heard my record all the way down in Shreveport," I said.

"It's playing everywhere we have distribution," Sam said, "and distribution is growing."

"No kidding," I responded, not having any idea what he meant. "Where all is that?"

"Texas, Florida, New Mexico, all across the South and Southeast," he said. "And we'll cover the whole country with *Folsom Prison Blues.*"

Fan mail had started coming in, and I would spread the letters out on the living room floor, counting the different states on the postmarks (nine in all the first time I did it, and much of it from the Shreveport area).

So the management asked me the minute I came offstage that night if I'd sign up as a regular member of the Hayride, to be there every Saturday night as a featured guest. I accepted. I felt by doing so I was going through another door that was opening for me. The Grand Ole Opry would be next, and not long in coming — another dream come true, another prayed-for achievement.

Backstage at the "Louisiana Hayride" had been like pandemonium. There seemed to be as many people backstage as out front. The dressing rooms were full of singers, musicians, and their friends, plus fans, promoters, agents, and a particular breed of free-hearted female that country entertainers called "snuff queens," who circulated among the musicians and singers.

Whiskey and beer were in every dressing room, and I must have been offered a drink a hundred times that night, but I wasn't drinking — yet.

The "Louisiana Hayride" had been the springboard of success for many great country artists such as Faron Young, Webb Pierce, and Hank Williams, and onstage with me were two others who were on their way, George Jones and Johnny Horton.

This was the first night I'd spent away from home since I'd been married, and Sunday morning, driving from Shreveport to Gladewater, Texas, something about it all didn't feel quite right. It didn't take many miles before I knew what it was.

The performance the night before had been an emotional "high." The wild enthusiasm of the audience had been stimulating. I had sung at a fever pitch, pouring all the energy I had into every song.

Now it was Sunday morning, and there was a little letdown in the naked light of day.

Marshall was driving the car, Luther was beside him in the front seat, and I was lying across the back seat. Every few minutes we'd have to slow down to allow cars to turn in to the churches all along the highway.

"That's why I feel so low this morning. I ought to be in church," I said.

"Do you want to go?" Marshall asked. "I'll stop at a church if you want to."

Luther turned around to look at me to see what my

answer would be. "I'll go with you," he said.

I didn't realize it, but my answer would establish a precedent, the beginning of a habit, a working pattern which would stand for years. My policy of aloneness and severed fellowship from other committed Christians would weaken me spiritually. Not that missing church necessarily meant missing God. It was just that Jesus never meant for us to try and make it on our own. There is something so important in worshiping together with other believers. And missing it would leave me vulnerable and easy prey for all the temptations and destructive vices that the backstage of the entertainment world has to offer.

I knew I needed to stop and get some spiritual feeding. If every night in this business was going to be like last night in Shreveport, I knew I'd need not just a weekly, but a daily dose of God.

But I laid back down in the seat. "Naw, let's go on down the road," I said. "We've got a show to do tonight."

In the dressing room at Gladewater I was sitting with Carl Perkins, strumming on the guitar, making "runs," "vamping," changing chords, and humming along with it.

"There was a doctor back home at Dyess named Hollingsworth," I said. "He hummed all the time. I always thought if Dr. Hollingsworth could have put his humming to music, he might have had a hit."

"What you're doing there sounds like a hit to me," Carl said.

"This is an idea I got today," I said. "I want to write a song that has something to *say*. A song that will have a lot of meaning not only for me, but for everybody who hears it — that says I'm going to be true not only to those who believe in me and depend on me, but to myself and to God — a song that might give courage to others as well as myself.''

   Carl said, ''That's a good idea. What will you call it?''

   ''I don't know,'' I said. ''Something like 'I'm Still Being True' or 'I'm Walking the Line' or some such thing.''

   ''*I Walk the Line* would be a good title,'' Carl said.

   ''Hmmmmmmmmmm —'' I began.

   The song came easily. It was one of those rare times I've felt a song was just ''begging to be written.'' There was no wringing the mind or biting the pencil on *I Walk the Line*. The lyrics came as fast as I could write, and in twenty minutes I had it finished.

> I keep a close watch on this heart of mine.
> I keep my eyes wide open all the time.
> I keep the ends out for the tie that binds.
> Because you're mine,
> I walk the line.

8 / A Demon Called "Deception"

National recognition came with the release of
I Walk the Line in 1956. *Folsom Prison Blues* had become
a country standard, but *I Walk the Line* was, and is, my
biggest selling record to date. It was a seller, as we like
to say, "in all fields."

After a year on the Hayride, I moved to the Grand
Ole Opry for two years, though guesting there only
occasionally because the concert tours took me away for
long periods of time.

Big television shows called. I appeared on Dick
Clark's "American Bandstand," with Ed Sullivan,
Jackie Gleason, Lawrence Welk, and on Red Foley's
"Ozark Jubilee."

I performed in every state in the Union, plus
tours across Canada and to Europe and the Far East.
Whether in the Palladium in London, Carnegie Hall,
New York, the Hollywood Bowl, or Pine Bluff, Arkansas,
I never did a concert that I didn't sing *I Walk the Line*.
And I never sang it that I didn't mean it, or that I
didn't *want* to mean it.

In 1958 I signed with Columbia Records and went
to Nashville and recorded two albums which were

released immediately. One was called (if you'll pardon the expression) "The Fabulous Johnny Cash." The other was an album of my favorite hymns and gospel songs.

The dream of recording an album of hymns was realized, but there wasn't the joy and fulfillment in it that I would have known earlier. The importance of a hymn album was minimized by so many in the record business that it had lost some of its importance to me; still, I had pledged to "tithe" my music.

But at this point in my career, I took a definite step in a wrong direction. I was on a tour with several Grand Ole Opry artists out of Nashville in 1957. Ferlin Husky and Faron Young were on the tour, and it was here I became close friends with Gordon Terry who worked with Faron.

We were driving in two cars that night to Jacksonville after the concert in Miami. Gordon was driving Faron's limousine, leading us, and about halfway to Jacksonville he pulled over and stopped, and we stopped behind him. We all got out of the cars, and Gordon walked over to Luther who was driving my car.

"Are you sleepy, Luther?" Gordon asked.

"I sure am," he said.

"Take one of these. It'll keep you awake." And he gave Luther a little white pill with a cross on it.

"What are they?" I asked Gordon.

"Bennies," he said.

"Will they hurt you?" I asked.

"I don't think so," said Gordon. "They've never hurt me. Here, have one. They'll make you want to go to Jacksonville and enjoy yourself after you get there."

I took one of the white pills and got in the car with Gordon. Within thirty minutes I felt refreshed, wide-awake, and talkative.

That night in Jacksonville, I still hadn't slept at show time. I got another pill from Gordon and did the show feeling great. It was the next night in another town before I finally "came down" from the two pills. They left me exhausted, but I had discovered something I sincerely thought would be a good thing for me.

With all the traveling I had to do, and upon reaching a city tired and weary, those pills could pep me up and make me really feel like doing a show. I got a handful of the little white ones from Gordon.

Those white pills were just one of a variety of a dozen or more shapes and sizes. Truck drivers used them as did people with the problem of being overweight. They called them amphetamines, Dexedrine, Benzedrine, and Dexamyl. They had a whole bunch of nice little names for them to dress them up, and they came in all colors. If you didn't like green, you could get orange. If you didn't like orange, you could get red. And if you really wanted to act like you were going to get weird, you could get black. Those black ones would take you all the way to California and back in a '53 Cadillac with no sleep.

Inside that bottle of white pills, which only cost eight or ten dollars for a hundred, came at no extra cost a demon called Deception.

For the first year or two when I took amphetamines on a fairly regular basis, I discovered newly expanded limits to my stamina and performing ability.

I've always loved to perform, but I've never gone onstage without experiencing those "butterflies" just as I am introduced. With a couple of pills in me, "bennies" as we called them, those butterflies didn't happen. Instead, I had courage and confidence.

At times when I first began using them, I honestly believed the bennies were God-sent to help me be a better performer. My energy was multiplied. My timing was superb. I enjoyed every song in every concert and could perform with a driving, relentless intensity. They stimulated the mind, made me think faster and talk more.

If I'd ever been shy before an audience, I wasn't any more. I rattled off my lines of dialogue between songs that kept people interested and entertained. I was personable, outgoing, energetic — I loved everybody!

So the deception was complete, and I used them more and more, until the time came in 1959 or '60 when I *had* to have them.

It was easy to get the pills most anywhere. At random I'd telephone a physician out of the Yellow Pages and say, "Doctor, this is Johnny Cash. I've got a long tour comin' up, and I gotta do a lot of night drivin'. I need some of those diet pills to keep me awake."

Back then I don't think the doctors themselves knew the danger of those pills because I never had any trouble getting them until 1963 or '64. After I got addicted to them, I'd go back to the same doctor for another prescription and say, "Maybe this time you could give me the ten-milligram tablets instead of the five, so I won't have to take but one at a time."

You learn all kinds of tricky little things like that. Your mind gets to conniving way down in the southeast corner to wring a little something else out of this doctor to get an extra kick here, an extra little something there. When you get on that stuff, you want something a little bit better, something a little bit bigger.

Sometimes I'd get so high, I'd be above my conscience, but when I came down it would still be there. From time to time I'd worry a bit that the pills were beginning to hurt me, but I'd take another pill and I wouldn't worry any more.

Before I really got hooked, I would realize what was happening and I'd think, "What am I doing to myself?" I think back now to interviews where questions would be coming, and I couldn't think of the answers.

Or, I'd be answering a question, and then all of a sudden right in the middle of it I'd forget what the question was. And I'd realize it was the pills. They regulated my mind and began to take control.

Everyone noticed the change the pills brought about in me. My friends made a joke out of my "nervousness." I had a twitch in the neck, the back, the face. My eyes dilated. I couldn't stand still. I twisted, turned, contorted, and popped my neck bones. It often felt like someone had a fist between my shoulder blades, twisting the muscle and bone, stretching my nerves, torturing them to the breaking point.

At home, my wife and children were often awakened by the sound of my banging around and walking the floor, trying to wear the pills out. More often they were awakened by the sound of my car starting as I was leaving to drive recklessly for hours through the streets and into the hills and deserts of California until I either wrecked the car or finally stopped from exhaustion.

In 1959 I had moved my family to California, and my break with church and a way of living and worshiping I had known since childhood was nearly complete. I fell right into the Southern California life style and made believe I was enjoying it. I even developed a taste for vodka, wine, and beer. I found you can cultivate a taste for anything as long as you keep on tasting.

The mixture of amphetamines and alcohol was a maddening poison, and I changed drastically. My wife and children feared the strange man I had become.

Depression followed the long periods of "highs." I was burdened down with guilt and prayed for strength to fight the habits that were taking control. My big mistake, however, was that I didn't turn it over to God. I held on to too much "man-pride," telling myself, "You're not so bad."

The demon called Deception had become a close companion. He never left me for long.

The drying agent in the amphetamines along with the cigarettes and alcohol brought on chronic laryngitis. The laryngitis lasted for days, then weeks.

At Carnegie Hall in New York City, I couldn't speak above a whisper. This concert was to be a milestone for me, and I had come to New York two days early to do interviews on radio and television.

One of the appearances I made was on the "Mike Wallace Show." I always kept myself on the defensive now. I knew people who were wise to the habit I was getting myself into, like Mike Wallace, would realize what was wrong with me through my twitchiness, dry mouth, and dilated eyes. I glared at Mike.

"Do you really like show business?" Mike asked me.

"It beats pickin' cotton," I shot back.

"What else did you do in Arkansas besides picking cotton?" he inquired.

"I killed snakes," I said with a wry smile, thinking I was being terribly clever.

"You look a little snaky yourself," Mike said.

"Watch out I don't strike you," I answered.

He quickly changed the subject.

"Why are you bringing country music to Carnegie Hall?" Mike asked.

"Why not?" I growled.

And the interview was ended.

The next night, my supporting acts, the Carter Family, Tompall and the Glaser Brothers, and Merle Kilgore, saved the evening for me. I could only whisper. And as hard as I tried, song after song for an hour, I couldn't sing.

The audience was disappointed, but accepted with reservation the M.C.'s explanation that I had a bad cold and laryngitis.

I found a dark corner backstage and sat there in deep depression. Mother Maybelle Carter and her daughters Helen, Anita, and June came back to try to cheer me up.

"We were praying for you out there tonight," June said.

"I'm afraid I wasn't praying with you," I whispered.

I had known Merle Kilgore since the late fifties. We had met at Johnny Horton's home before Johnny was killed in an auto accident in 1960. My friendship with Kilgore continued. He and I had started taking pills at about the same time, although they affected us differently.

I became intensely active, nervous, restless, and after awhile destructive — not only destroying furniture and cars, but abusing myself by staying on them for days without sleep.

Kilgore got happy when he took them. He talked a mile a minute. He liked everybody, and everybody liked him. At times he was mysteriously quiet, at times spiritualistic. He was full of fun, and he tried a little of everything.

"Let me hypnotize you," he said to me one night after a concert.

"OK," I said. "What do I do?"

"Look into my eyes," said Kilgore.

I stared.

"When I count to three, you'll close your eyes, and you can't open them," Merle said.

I stared.

"One . . . two . . . three . . . close."

I clamped my eyes shut.

"Now listen to me, Cash," he said, "you are going into a deep trance . . . deeper . . . deeper . . . deeper. Now you are in a deep trance."

I was having trouble keeping my eyes closed because of the bennies, but I squeezed them tight.

"We are going to see if you lived in a previous

life," said Merle. "You are going back in time now . . .
back . . . back . . . back . . . to before you were born. Now
keep your eyes closed and concentrate. What do you
see? What do you feel?"

I could hear the excitement in his voice, so I
thought I'd go along with it for a little fun.

"It's warm and damp in here," I said.

"Wow! No kidding!" he said. "Now listen, Cash.
We are going deeper and deeper. A very deep trance.
Deeper . . . deeper . . . back into the past. Now tell me, what
do you see? What do you feel? Who are you?"

I paused a long time, milking the situation. Finally
I said, "I'm a Hebrew slave in Egypt." (I had just seen
the movie *The Ten Commandments*.)

"Wow! In Egypt? Well, uh, let me think. What
can you tell me? Hey! Who is Pharaoh?"

"Mmmm, I don't know," I said. "We just call
him Pharaoh."

"What are you doing?" Merle said, getting wise.

I opened one eye and peeped at Merle. "Making
mud bricks," I said.

"You're lying to me, Cash," he said.

"I'm sorry, Kilgore," I said. "I can't go into a
trance."

"OK," he said. "But let's don't play around
with that stuff any more."

The longer I took pills, the more unpredictable and
violent I got. Merle couldn't understand that in me. I
went to his apartment dozens of nights, waking him up,
needing someone to talk to. As time went by and I got in
worse shape, I sensed a change in Merle toward me.

He had tried to tolerate me and my intrusions on
his privacy, my invasion of his home, but I made such a
nuisance of myself that I began to find him "not at home."
Finally, I avoided him purposely myself because I had
gone so low that I was ashamed to face him most of the
time.

In Las Vegas months later where I took a week's engagement in the lounge of a small downtown hotel, Tompall and the Glaser Brothers again carried most of the show. The amphetamines, alcohol, cigarettes coupled with the dry air of Nevada took my voice again. Each night I became weaker and with the continued use of the drug lost sight of my obligation to my audience.

As I was leaving my room to go to the lounge on the fourth night, I answered a knock at the door. There stood Roger Miller.

"I'm doing your show for you tonight," he said.

"Who says so?" I asked.

"I do," said Roger. "You're not able."

"How do you know I'm not?" I whispered.

"Sing *Folsom Prison Blues* for me," said Roger.

"I'll sing it all right," I said.

"Go ahead and try. You can't."

"I can."

"Dare you."

"Don't worry about me, Roger," I said. "I can do my show. I've never had to have anybody take my place yet."

"Now wait a minute, oh fabulous one," said Roger. "I'm your friend, remember? I am one of the all-time great authorities on pillology, and Roger says the fabulous one will rest tonight."

"Who called you about me, Roger? Tompall?" I asked.

"No," he said, skirting around the answer. "It's my Indian blood. I said to myself, 'Roger,' I said, 'your brother, Running Dilating Cash, has that lean, hungry, dry look. Go,' I said. 'Go to yon hellhole in the desert and relieve the great whispering one.' "

"Thanks for coming, Roger," I said. "Maybe I can do the same for you sometime."

"Don't count it a debt," he said, "and I won't." And off he went to the lounge to take my place.

Roger Miller relieved me that night and the next and the next and the next. Then he drove me home to California.

By now I had been a regular on the Grand Ole Opry for a couple of years, and from time to time up to 1965 I appeared as special guest. But I stayed on the road most of the time working one long concert tour after another.

Occasionally I was missing show dates because of the laryngitis, and I canceled nine out of every ten recording sessions my producer booked.

One Saturday night, in Nashville for an appearance on the Grand Ole Opry, I arrived at the Ryman Auditorium having taken the pills regularly for weeks. My voice was gone as were a few more pounds of body weight. I was down to about 165. That nightmare appearance brought me to a sobering realization of what I was doing to myself.

The band kicked off a song, and I tried to take the microphone off the stand. In my nervous frenzy, I couldn't get it off. Such a minor complication in my mental state was enough to make me explode in a fit of anger. I took the mike stand, threw it down, then dragged it along the edge of the stage, popping fifty or sixty footlights. The broken glass shattered all over the stage and into the audience.

The song ended abruptly, and I walked offstage and came face to face with the Grand Ole Opry manager. He kindly and quietly informed me, "We can't use you on the Opry any more, John."

I couldn't answer. I had sobered again in the time it took to blink.

I walked out the back door of the Grand Ole Opry house, got in my car, and started driving. After a few blocks, I headed south through the residential areas to

avoid police cars out on the highway. I was crying now,
and I couldn't see well enough to drive.

It began to rain, and as I reached to turn on the
windshield wipers, the car swerved and crashed into a
tree beside the street.

I woke up in the emergency room at the hospital
with a broken nose and a broken jaw. The car was totaled out.

A friend of mine, Columbia Records man Gene
Ferguson, came and got me and took me home with him
to recuperate.

9 / **Strange Voices**

On my way to Chicago for an appearance at Soldiers' Field several months later, a young man introduced himself to me.

"I'm Charlie Pride," he said. "I sing country, too, and I've always wanted to meet you."

I had heard of Charlie Pride from Jack Clement who had "discovered" him and was producing his records. One of his first records, *Just Between You and Me,* had gained him some solid recognition in the country music field.

"Are you working in town tonight?" I asked.

"Yeah," he said. "I'm playing a spot called the Rivoli Club. But I'm not sure how it will work out — I don't suppose they've ever had a black man singing there before."

(And I thought *I* had had tough doors to open. I couldn't imagine what it was like for Charlie Pride, even with his talent.)

"Just sing it the way you feel it, Charlie, and you won't go wrong," I advised. "By the way, how late do you work? Maybe I could come by and see you after I finish."

"About 1:30 in the morning," he said. "Sure would be glad to see you."

"Where are you staying?" I asked. "I'll call you later and let you know."

He gave me the name of his motel, and we separated with, "I'll see you later."

I had been alert and sober when I met Charlie Pride that evening, but by the time I finished my engagement at 10:30 P.M., I was just getting set to begin for the night. I returned to the hotel, got a night's supply of pills, a briefcase full of beer, my guitar, and headed out to find Charlie.

When I went to tell the friendly black cab driver where I wanted to go, I couldn't recall the name of the club. "Do you know of a place that features country music called the Trivoli or Rivoli or Riviera or some such name?" I asked.

He said, "I know 'em all. Which one do you want?"

"Let's try all of them. There's a black country-western singer named Charlie Pride who is playing at one of them, and I want to see him."

The driver turned and looked at me. "You're putting me on, man!"

"Let's try them," I said.

He lit a marijuana joint and offered it to me.

"No thank you," I said.

"Aw, come on, man. You're *on* something. A little grass ain't gonna hurt."

"How do you know I'm on something?" I asked.

" 'It takes one to know one,' they say," he smiled, as he offered me the joint again.

This time I took it, and we passed it back and forth until it was gone. I had tried marijuana perhaps a half-dozen times before, but only when I was already high on pills. So I never was able to know its real effect on me.

We stopped in front of a club. "Is this the one?" the driver asked.

The sign on the door said: *In Person – Sister Rosetta Tharpe.*

"No, but this one will do for now," I said. "Come on in with me. I've got to see Sister Rosetta."

The driver and I walked in, sat down, and each ordered a beer. The bandstand was quiet, in-between "sets." An all-black audience had packed the place out, waiting for the next show. And before long Sister Rosetta came on stage and began with *This Train.*

> This train is bound for glory, this train.
> This train is bound for glory, this train.
> This train is bound for glory,
> Nobody rides it but the righteous and the holy.
> This train is bound for glory, this train.

"Hey, man. What are you crying for?" my driver asked as he looked over at me.

"I don't know," I said. "I guess she just got to me with that song."

I took a couple more pills, washing them down with the beer, while she finished her set with *There Are Strange Things Happening Every Day.* And as we were walking out, the driver said matter-of-factly to me, "You're Johnny Cash."

I didn't answer him.

"Let's go back in and let me introduce you to Sister Rosetta, man. She'd be glad to meet you," he said.

"Not tonight she wouldn't," I said as I got in the cab. My vision had begun to blur; the lights and the sounds around me were strange and distorted.

"Bennies, beer, and pot," I told the driver. "Something in the combination isn't working well."

He lit another joint and passed it back. "This will clear your head," he said.

The next thing I remember was him saying, "It's 2:00 A.M. You want me to keep looking for that club?"

"No," I said, suddenly remembering where Charlie Pride was staying. "Stop at this phone booth."

"Charlie," I said, "it's Cash. I tried to find that club and couldn't. I'll come on over to the motel, OK?"

"Uh — well — I was just lying down, and — what time is it?" he stammered.

"It's early yet," I said. "I'll be right over." And I hung up.

Arriving at the motel, I grabbed my guitar and briefcase from inside the cab, paid the driver, and headed for Charlie's room. He was up out of bed and dressed. I think he knew he was in for a long evening.

"Want a beer?" I asked, opening up my briefcase.

"No thanks," said Charlie.

"How'd it go at the club?" I inquired, taking my guitar out of the case.

"Pretty good," he said. "I'm about sung out."

"Let's swap songs," I insisted.

"You sing one," he said. "Really, I'm about sung out."

So I sang one, then another, then another. I had all these sheets of long, yellow paper I carried in my briefcase with the beer. The songs were in various stages of completion. Most of them never would be finished because they were begun in the same condition in which I was now trying to sing them. My mind would go off in another direction before I ever got the songs written.

I took a couple more pills and kept playing. But I didn't offer Charlie any pills. With him being new in the music business, I figured he wouldn't even know about them. Anyway, like the cab driver had said, "It takes one to know one." And I thought that it also took one to know one who is *not*. Charlie Pride, I felt, was not one who would share my poison.

He was considerate as he lay back on his pillow listening to me, trying to stay awake.

"Listen to this one," I'd say, and at the end he would compliment me.

"Man, that's a good song," he'd say. And he and I both knew better.

Finally, Charlie sang a couple songs for me. By now, he had no doubt given up as lost the idea of going to bed at all, and I suppose he felt compelled to "swap songs" after all.

"That's good," I said. "You're one of the best country singers I've ever heard. You're going to be big, Charlie."

"I don't know, John," he said. "At least I've got a recording contract and an album on the way. But there are other things I want to do."

"Like what?" I asked.

"Well, one thing is I've always wanted to sing on the Grand Ole Opry, but I don't know if they'd ever let me."

Without knowing it, Charlie had touched a shamefully sensitive spot with me. There had been no publicity on my being "banned" from the Opry. I had simply been informed quietly, "We can't use you any more, Cash." Charlie doesn't know about that, I thought.

Then I did something I had learned to do very well when on pills and alcohol: I started lying. And once I started, I couldn't stop.

"I'll get you on the Opry, Charlie," I volunteered.

"No kidding," he said. "Will you?"

"Sure," I said, getting excited about it with him and making myself forget my own estranged position with the Opry. "The next time I play there, I'll just tell them you're my guest and that they'll have to let you sing."

"When are you going to be on again?" he asked.

"I don't know, but pretty soon," I assured him, lying through my teeth. "I'll let you know in a few weeks, but you can plan on it."

"Well," he said thoughtfully, "it might not be as easy as you think."

"Man, don't worry about it," I said. "Consider it done. You belong on the Opry, and I'm going to take you with me next time I'm on."

I was telling the truth on one score — Charlie had the talent and belonged on the Opry and on any country show. But I immediately began hating myself for playing the big shot and leading him on.

The sun was coming up, and the talk about the Opry had brought me down.

"Are you sleepy yet?" Charlie asked me.

"No, but I guess I'd better let you get some rest," I said. "I'll call a cab to my hotel."

"I can't let you do that," he said, putting on his shoes. "I have a rented car downstairs. I'll take you."

We hit the Chicago morning rush hour right at its peak, and it was 8:30 or 9:00 before we reached the hotel.

"I'll call you about the Opry," I said guiltily, but firmly unwilling to give up the lie.

"Just take care of yourself and get some rest. We need you, John." Charlie smiled as he closed the door to drive away.

I walked into my room and immediately closed the curtains to keep out the strong morning light. With a half-glass of water I chased a handful of tranquilizers to put me out, and I laid down.

The "downers" wiped out any remaining guilt I had over lying, and as I lay there somewhere between consciousness and oblivion, I remember thinking, "What did Charlie Pride mean when he said, 'We need you, John'?"

Between tours the battles continued to rage at

home. In my agitated mental state, fighting came easily for me. Coping with me while I was on drugs became an impossible task for Vivian.

The demon called Deception always went with me. I took the amphetamines "just in case I need them."

Deception said, "Take your barbiturates, too, so you can get some rest." So I took both kinds of pills — and beer — and headed for the mountains or desert to "rest." Once in the mountains, I never rested. Night followed day, then another day, then another night with no sleep.

The mixture of the two drugs plus alcohol opened the door of my mind and let all the demons in to join Deception.

The furies literally clawed at my brain. Every move of every muscle was torture from the days and nights of abuse. My nerves were at a screaming breaking point.

One night I drove my jeep across a salt flat and up a long, arid hillside, zigzagging around mesquite and manzanita until I reached the top. I couldn't see over the other side.

"I dare you to turn off your lights and go down the other side," I said to me.

"Let me have a beer first," I answered me.

I drank one, then another.

"What have I got to lose?" I said, as I stood up in the jeep and started down the side, crying, clenching my fists, and holding on to the steering wheel.

The jeep started picking up speed. I hit a few bushes, then some more, then bigger ones. The small trees and boulders slowed me down, but I was staying upright.

By moonlight I could see I was speeding down through an open clearing, and darkness lay straight ahead. That darkness turned out to be a thick grove of

manzanita bushes and trees which I crashed into and
through at full speed, and I dropped down into the seat to
keep the limbs from knocking me out. The jeep fairly
flew out of the grove and onto level ground on the other side
and finally stopped.

I couldn't turn loose of the steering wheel. My
knuckles were white, and it was like my bony hands were
welded to the wheel. I was in an icy sweat, cold-sober now
and shaking.

It was a long time before I stopped crying and gave
up and went back home.

I had a good friend in Ventura County named
Curly Lewis. He had a construction company, and he built
my house in Casitas Springs. On some of my first "escapes"
to the mountains and deserts in my camper, he accompanied
me. At first on overnight or weekend trips, Curly would
stay up all night with me, and we hunted and prowled in the
mountains and deserts all the way to Death Valley. I was
strangely fascinated by the desert and especially by Death
Valley when I was taking pills. The name itself fascinated
me — I suppose because I knew deep down inside that if I
continued with the drugs, death would be my lot.

After a few such trips, Curly wouldn't stay up all
night with me. He slept in the back of the camper while I
walked around the desert alone all night with a gun and a
light, returning to the camper occasionally for beer or
whatever I was drinking along with the pills. I think
Curly knew I was taking amphetamines, but sensing that I
was trying to hide it from him, he never mentioned it to me.

I asked my daddy to go along with us on one of
these overnight trips. Late that night in the Mojave Desert I
drove the camper at full speed right through a gate and a
sign that read: "No trespassing. U. S. Naval Proving
Grounds — U.S.N. Ordinance."

"What's the navy doing out here?" I asked.

"I don't know, but I have a feeling we're going to get into trouble," my daddy said.

After a few miles of rough, washed-out, dirt road, we came upon a long stretch of pavement, and I headed down it. It was puzzling. Fifty miles from the nearest house or highway, and here was a highway straight as an arrow going who knows where. But when we saw the bomb holes and pieces of destroyed military vehicles, we suddenly knew what it was.

"We're on a bombing and strafing range!" said Curly. "Look at the bomb and bullet holes in the pavement."

He was right. We started dodging holes and pieces of shrapnel and vehicles that were lying all over the pavement.

"They probably send the trucks and jeeps and tanks down this road by remote control and the planes practice blowing them up and shooting at them," Curly said. Then we saw a flashing light miles ahead, apparently trying to signal us. "Uh, oh," daddy said, "I told you we were going to get into trouble in here. I'm afraid the navy has got us now."

"Don't worry about it," I said. "We'll tell them we got lost."

"Well, that might work unless they know you busted through that gate," daddy said.

The pavement ended abruptly, and we continued weaving our way toward the flashing light steadily coming our way. It was a military vehicle. "Follow me," said the navy man as he approached us with a rifle aimed our way.

"It's been almost fifty years since I saw a military stockade, and I've never seen a navy brig, but I think we are about to," said daddy.

We followed the military vehicle out another gate where we stopped and all got out. The navy man said, as he approached us, "There are hundreds, maybe thousands, of dud bombs and land mines out there. I fully expected to see you blow up before I could get to you." He asked for our identification, and after he took our names and addresses, I asked him, "Are we free to go?"

"For the time being," he said. "Don't come back on government property."

That trip had been a close call in a lot of ways, so I gave up and took my daddy and Curly back home to Ventura County. We expected to hear from the navy or the government or somebody over the incident, but we never did.

Daddy didn't make any more trips to the mountains or deserts with me, and after a while neither did Curly Lewis. I am sure they were convinced I would die out there some night. Curly and I continued to be friends, and he often came by or called when I was at home, but he left me to go off alone on my escapades.

For many periods of one and two weeks over those seven drugged years, I was completely straight and trying again. For awhile I was a member of the Avenue Community Church in Ventura, California, where I lived from 1961 to 1966. Floyd Gressett was the pastor there. I joined the church and again made a rededication stand. I tried hard for awhile to overcome the drugs and did for brief intervals, but the drugs had a stronger hold on me.

It was like a New Year's resolution kind of commitment. It was mere temporary reform. I knew I'd pushed everybody, including myself, to the breaking point, and all I really wanted was a breather.

So I held on to that pride of self. To repent and reform all the way to righteousness requires a man to first recognize and admit he has been all wrong. To make such a change as I needed, and to be able to say, "I'm going to be right from now on," I was also required to say, "I've been all wrong up to now." And I didn't care to admit that.

Rev. Floyd Gressett had a small ranch in the mountains, and I often went up there alone, or at times with him.

He and I had a strange understanding which was the only way I would allow his friendship with me to exist. I had to make-believe he didn't know I was hooked on pills. And though he did know, he had to act like he didn't. He saw me at times when I was staggering, stumbling, and mumbling from exhaustion. He came looking for me more than once and found me at the point of death from days without food. He'd take me back to the ranch and give me food and a bed, and usually some word from home to remind me in a kind way of my obligations there. But he handled me carefully so as not to alienate me.

As time went by and the habit took firmer control, I learned that with a few more pills even my grief and guilt would bother me no more. So for all practical purposes, my girls lost a daddy, and their daddy was coming closer and closer to losing his mortal and spiritual life.

Floyd Gressett was always kind to me, even when I was at my worst. But he was wise enough to know from having preached for thirteen years in the prisons of California that a man taking drugs isn't going to listen to you. And if he's acting like he's listening, he's very likely not listening. And I wasn't listening — not yet.

I know that the hand of God was never off me, no matter what condition I was in, for there is no other way to explain my escaping the many, many accidents I had. Besides wrecking every car I had for seven years, I totaled two jeeps and a camper and turned over two tractors and a bulldozer. I sank two boats in separate accidents on a lake, and I jumped from a truck just before it went over a six-hundred-foot cliff in California.

In the wild, nervous frenzy the amphetamines produced, I could never catch up with all the things that my mind in its artificially stimulated excitement could think

of to do. I had to build things, and I'm not a carpenter. I
had to fix things. I took my guitars apart and couldn't glue
them back together right. I would stay up all night
writing letters to people I hardly knew; luckily, I usually
reread them in a sober light and never mailed them.

The potent mixture of amphetamines and alcohol
coupled with days and nights without sleep bent my mind
in a stranger direction. I began to hear voices. I couldn't
understand what was being said, but I knew they were
talking to me.

The first couple of times it happened I sobered and
was a little afraid. One time, however, after being up on
the desert for two or three days and nights living solely on
amphetamines and beer, I took tranquilizers in an effort
to come down, and muscle spasms covered my body. I
turned my jeep towards the ranch house about five
miles away. It was night, and Rev. Gressett was asleep at
the ranch.

I hadn't gone over two miles when I heard a voice
yelling my name. I stopped the jeep and turned off the
motor and headlights.

I yelled, "Hello."

Nobody answered.

I started the jeep and heard the voice again. I
turned the motor off.

"Speak up!" I said.

No answer.

"Who are you?" I yelled.

I sat quietly for a minute. Then a voice came out of
me, but it wasn't my voice.

I grinned and turned wildly around in the jeep and
said, "Speak up!"

Then the next voice that came out of me I
recognized. "Have another bennie," Deception said.
"Those tranquilizers are making you sleepy."

"No," growled another voice out of me. "I'm
about dead."

"Dead?" said the first voice. "Nothing can kill you."

I reached my hand in my pocket and brought out my bennies. ". . . nine, ten, eleven, twelve in all," I counted aloud. "I had a hundred two days ago."

A voice said, "You must have lost some."

I washed down two of them with what was left of a can of warm beer.

When I got to the ranch house, I sat down on the front porch. The bennies were doing their work now, and the voices were quiet — a calm, dangerous quiet.

Across the field in the moonlight was a huge, old oak tree. It was hollow and occupied by a swarm of bees. The last time I'd been to the ranch I'd tried to rob the bees of their honey. In the process I suffered about forty bee stings and never got a drop of honey.

"The bees are all asleep right now," I thought. "I could take my logging chain, tie the end to the frame underneath the back of my jeep, tie the other end around one of the big branches near the truck, and break it down. Then it would be easier to get the honey."

I managed to get the chain attached without arousing the bees. I bolted the other end underneath the back frame of the jeep. Then I surveyed the situation. "This will do it," I said aloud. "You bees are going to get paid back now." I was laughing as I sat down behind the steering wheel and started the motor. I shoved it in four-wheel drive, jammed the gas pedal to the floor, and popped out the clutch. When the logging chain straightened out, the jeep stopped, but I kept going.

When I woke up, I was lying twenty feet in front of the jeep flat on the ground. Rev. Gressett was pouring water on my head. He was trying to keep from laughing, and he controlled it until he saw I was all right. Then he couldn't help it. I had been knocked out cold as I flattened

the hinged windshield, flew over the front of the jeep,
and landed on my head.

He finally got me to the ranch house, and I headed
for bed. Just as I was about to go to sleep, he said, "You
can thank the Lord for one thing, John."

"What's that?" I asked.

"You didn't wake up the bees."

Though I kept company with those demons and
allowed them to court me, badger me, hassle me, and
taunt me, they could never claim me. Friends, loved ones,
casual acquaintances, and even fans who didn't know me
personally but knew my problem and cared for me were
praying for me all across the country. These faithful people
were claiming the promises in His name that as one of His
children I would come through and someday be all right.

Many times after a long period of being up and high
for days, when I would finally calm down and give in to
rest, when the raging voices quieted and the evil presences
left me, there would move in gently about me a warm,
sweet presence, and a still, small voice would breathe forth
inside my being: "I am your God. I am still here. I am
still waiting. I still love you."

And I would sleep.

10 / **Pocket Full of Pills**

At the end of 1966, I had been staying in Nashville most of the time between tours. I grieved for my little girls in California. Things were beyond repair in my home. I had gone too far, stayed away too much. Too many bonds were broken. The girls grieved for me also, but it was harder and harder to face them each time I saw them. There could be no repairing much of the damage that had been done, even if I was strong enough and straight enough to try.

I tried to go home to see them that year at Christmas time. I left Nashville on December 20, and it was Christmas Eve before I arrived in California. Everywhere the plane stopped, I got off and went to the clubs and honky-tonks, mixing with the kind of people who shared my particular brand of death. I spent two nights in Dallas, making all the clubs, sitting in with the musicians, drinking with them and taking pills.

Then I made it to Tucson and Phoenix and another whirlwind of clubs and bad company. Only the realization that it was Christmas Eve got me back on a plane to California.

The reaction to my arrival at home was one of surprise. They had given up hope that I'd be home for Christmas. There was no joy in the reunion, no Christmas spirit. I was like a stranger. I felt like one, and I knew I looked like one.

Vivian had already filed for divorce, and I was not contesting it. It would be a few more months until, according to California law, it would be final. But the marriage had already ended.

My parents lived just a few miles away near Ojai, and I spent some time with them. They tried to bring up the subject of salvaging my marriage "for the children's sake," but they never got a reasonable conversation off the ground with me. I was too weak emotionally to follow through on any such idea, even if I had been willing to discuss it, and they realized the situation was unalterable.

Christmas came and went, and I spent most of my time alone in the guest bedroom. I heard the girls laughing and playing, opening their presents. "Daddy is sick . . . daddy is tired."

I sensed the gulf I had caused between them and myself. Little children forgive and forget, but I'd never forget the things I missed sharing in their young lives — the million little precious things that happened while "daddy was on the road": Tara losing her first tooth; Cindy's piano recital; a first communion; Rosanne in the senior play; Kathy's birthday party; Rosanne's birthday party; Cindy and Tara's birthday party; an Easter egg hunt.

And the million important things that *they* would miss: a daddy to encourage them, a daddy to comfort them, a daddy to advise, teach, direct, protect, and love them.

The gulf was much more than I could fathom, much less have strength and wisdom enough to bridge. So the day after Christmas I returned to Nashville.

By now I was missing not just a concert or two because of the laryngitis, but, realizing my inability to do a good performance, I was canceling whole tours. Usually the promoters canceled the tours, but a couple of times, with big advance ticket sales, the promoters would refuse to cancel and I'd find out later that the rest of the show had performed without me, making excuses for my being "sick."

The Statler Brothers, who were a part of my show, laughed about my pills at first; then as things got worse I made believe the Statlers didn't even know about them — to the point that I actually made *myself* believe they didn't know. Harold Reid of the Statlers kidded about it occasionally before it got to be a taboo subject around me, but there came a time when my people were afraid to mention pills.

One morning after being up all night, I joined my group in the hotel lobby where we were gathering to leave.

"Are you sleepy, chief?" Harold asked me.

"No, I had some coffee," I said.

"You look sleepy," said Harold. "What I mean is, it seems to me if you could get your eyes to close, you might be sleepy."

"I didn't sleep a wink all night," I said. "I've got muscle spasms in my back."

"You look nervous, too," he said.

"I'm not nervous. I'm quick," I said.

"You don't require a lot of rest, do you?" asked Harold.

"I get my rest," I said. "I'll make it all right."

"You look sleepy to me," said Harold. "You sure you ain't sleepy, chief?"

As we walked out of the lobby to get on the bus, Harold put his arm around me and said, "Chief, you let us know if you ever get sleepy, and we'll try to have you a bed ready."

And so the kidding went on. There was and is a lot of love and care in my show cast. The Statlers and the Tennessee Three all let me know that they cared what happened to me.

Besides the Statler Brothers and the Tennessee Three, the Carter Family often accompanied me as I toured. June Carter started working as a featured attraction on my show in the early sixties. The one person who could get to me and talk to me when no one else could was June Carter, and everybody knew it. And when the pill habit got really bad, she started fighting it because she could see what it was doing to me.

As time went by, she noticed a difference in my performances — the unnatural energy and intensity I put into everything and the cold sweat and pale look afterwards.

Mother Maybelle Carter and June's sisters, Helen and Anita, who worked with us as the Carter Family, tried to stay out of my way and just do their job. When they'd catch me in a mood in which they thought I might be receptive, they'd offer me something to eat, or a glass of milk, or one of them would offer to press my shirt for me before going on stage — any kindness they could think of to let me know they cared.

But June Carter went farther. In the name of God, she claimed my recovery which she began fighting to bring about. She learned my habits, knew where I kept my pills, and when things got bad she would get them and throw them away. She would always tell me when she did, but she'd try to tell me after I had some sleep so I'd be in a better frame of mind to listen.

Sometimes I'd say, "I'm glad you threw them away. They're killing me." Other times I'd be angry and resentful. I'd shout at her and tell her to mind her own business, that she had no right.

Once I told her, "If you weren't a woman, I'd break your neck."

She looked me in the eye and smiled and said, "You'd miss me."

June was never afraid of me, and she was serious about the battle she was waging against the pills. "I'm just trying to help," she'd say. "God has His hand on you, and I'm going to try to help you become what you are whether you want me to or not."

When I was thinking straight, I agreed with her. And many times we'd go find an open church and pray. But those sessions did not produce that big change I needed. It was no complete surrender. It was not a total turning back to God. Even as I'd leave the church, that gnawing awareness would be present in my conscience that I had secret reservations.

Sometimes I'd call a hotel house doctor and get diet pills over the phone. I had lost so much weight that if I asked for diet pills from a doctor face to face, I knew he'd refuse.

So I'd use my name and say, "Doctor, this is Johnny Cash. I'm in town for a concert tonight. We've been doing a lot of traveling, a lot of night driving. I need something to keep me awake on some of these long trips. If you could give me a prescription for something that would be safe, like five-milligram Dexamyl tablets —"

"Certainly, Mr. Cash. How long a tour are you on?"

"Well, I guess it will run for about another six weeks." (I never had a tour over three weeks long in my life.)

And he'd say, "Well, let me see, how many do you think you'll need?"

I'd say, "Better give me fifty, maybe a hundred. I don't know. Do you think it would be all right if I got a hundred, doctor?"

"Certainly, I'll send them right over."

By the next day, I would have taken fifteen to twenty of those pills. So I'd have the same conversation with another doctor. If it didn't work with him, I'd call another one.

Or I'd call downstairs and ask the assistant manager if they had a doctor on call. Sometimes I'd get him to make the call for me, and the assistant manager calling on Mr. Cash's behalf would almost cinch my getting the pills.

Or I would call a doctor and suggest, "Why don't you just come to the concert tonight, and I'll get tickets for you. Bring the pills backstage."

These were the things June learned to fight. If we were at a concert and somebody would introduce a doctor to me backstage, she would immediately suspect I had called for a prescription and that he was bringing it to me. If she suspected a visitor was a doctor, she'd say, "Hi! I'm June Carter. Are you a doctor? I see your bag."

My temper would rise while she sweet-talked him, getting all the information as fast as she could. And could she get it!

"We're glad to have you, doctor. This is Johnny Cash. How are you, doctor?"

"I've met him, June," I'd fume.

The doctor would say, "Well, Mr. Cash, I've got —"

And June would interrupt. "Is anybody sick here tonight?"

I'd say, "Doctor, if you'd like to come into the dressing room —"

And June would agree, "Yes, come on in. John, let's all go in and sit down and take a breather."

I'd say, "Well, June, we'll see you later."

She'd pretend not to hear. "What is the trouble, John?"

"Oh, nothing," I'd answer. "I was just going to talk with the doctor."

"About what, John? What are you going to talk to him about?"

"Nothing."

"Are you sick?"

"June, I know what I'm doing. Get out."

"I see. Maybe you can get a prescription for Dexedrine, John."

And she'd turn around broken-hearted, surrendering, because she'd played the scene as long as she could play it.

I'd call June up later and say, "What are you doing?"

"I'm reading this Gideon Bible."

And I'd say, "What are you reading in the Bible?"

She'd quote me something that directly applied to my situation. It was like she'd been hoping I'd call so she could give me that Scripture. She didn't preach. She didn't sit down and say, "John, I want to read to you from the Bible." She'd make me ask, and she knew how to make me ask, for those words of life. She knew at what point in my death to make me want to reach out for life. She played it like a chess player, and I knew who was going to win.

Ezra Carter, June's father, and her mother, Maybelle, offered me their best room when I was back in Nashville and tried to keep me away from the wrong crowd of pill-heads and boozers. They didn't approve of my pills, but even when they knew I was on them they were kind to me and always let me know they believed in me.

They gave me a key to their house which I promptly lost, and coming home with no key and nobody there, I'd kick down a door to get in. Usually I'd fix the door once I was inside, but after awhile all the doors were splintered beyond repair and many windows were broken from being forced open.

I never could stand a locked door. To me it was a symbol of God's rejection and disapproval of what I was being at the time. I'd knock on a door, any door, and if there was no answer, I'd try the knob. If it was locked, I'd kick it open.

In more sober moments I realized how badly I was abusing my friends' good natures, and I finally rented an apartment in nearby Madison, Tennessee. It was a one-bedroom place with a kitchen and living room. My first night there alone I walked the floor until dawn. "This isn't the answer," I thought, "getting away by myself when I can't *stand* myself."

Next day in downtown Nashville I ran into Waylon Jennings who'd just come to town. "If you're looking for an apartment," I said, "why don't you move out there with me? I'll get them to put up another bed."

Waylon came out and looked. "Man, you're the worst housekeeper I ever saw. What have you been doing in the kitchen, fighting?"

"I cooked breakfast," I said. "Biscuits and gravy."

"Do me a favor and don't ever cook me any," Waylon said.

Waylon moved in with me, but I rarely saw him. He was in town all day and every night.

I had a large supply of Benzedrine, as well as hundreds of barbiturate pills. "Now I've got to hide these from Waylon," I thought. (I was telling myself now that Waylon wouldn't know I took pills.) Under the refrigerator, in the upholstery of the couch, in the bedding — I hid them wherever I could. I pulled baseboards off and hid them in the walls. And I always forgot immediately where I hid them.

I was frantically looking for the pills one night when Waylon came in. I had the air conditioner out of the window and was taking it apart to look inside when he walked in.

"What in the world are you doing?" he asked.

"I'm trying to fix this air conditioner," I said.

"See if you can find any pills in there while you're at it," Waylon grinned.

"Smart aleck," I thought. "I bet he's got pills himself."

Waylon went to bed and went to sleep. I hadn't found any of my pills, and I had to have some. So I went out to Waylon's car, and sure enough — the glove compartment was locked. "That's where he keeps them," I thought. I got a screwdriver and started prying the door off the compartment. I rammed the screwdriver in the crack and pulled hard. The tough, brittle plastic door shattered into a million pieces, and I looked inside, pulling papers, letters, tapes, everything but pills, out onto the floor.

I went back inside and went to bed, prepared to face Waylon whenever he discovered what I'd done. But Waylon never mentioned that busted glove compartment to me, and the fact he didn't was another thing that brought me to a sobering, awakening period.

If he had only gotten mad and tried to jump on me, I could have taken it. A good fight or argument was my way of life. I had it all figured out — I was going to get fighting mad and resentfully deny it when he came in and accused me of breaking into his glove compartment. Day after day passed, and still no mention of it, but I thought I saw a change in him. He was a little more aloof than before, I thought, a little more "superior" or something. And that *really* bothered me. "He knows I did it," I thought, "and he's not going to confront me with it." One time I planned to bring it up to him and apologize, but he went his way and I went mine.

"There goes another friendship," I thought. "Not

many bridges left to burn.'' But Waylon was too big a man to hold that against me. A couple of weeks later we sat in the living room, writing and singing.

"John," he said, "why do you stay in this little apartment when you could afford to buy a mansion?"

"I don't know," I said. "I guess I'd feel guilty about buying another house with my girls in California."

"Get yourself a nice house and maybe their mother will let them come visit you," he said.

"I'll see you later," I said.

I got in my car and drove east, out Gallatin Road and through Hendersonville.

"Maybe Waylon's got something there," I thought. "Stop leaning on other people. Get out of that apartment and get a place of my own. Maybe I can stop acting like a bum if I can stop living like one."

The country in Sumner County, past Hendersonville, is beautiful rolling hills, beef and dairy farms, tobacco patches, some nice homes, and Old Hickory Lake. This is Andrew Jackson country, the lake being named for "Old Hickory" himself. Across the lake was "The Hermitage," and in these fields and meadows he had hunted and rode his horses.

I passed "Rock Castle," the house where Rachel lived when she jumped from the window to elope with Jackson.

I turned off the highway and took a winding road down toward the lake. I drove into the area where I had been shown the homes of several entertainers and friends in my business. I passed Red Foley's house, Roy Acuff's, Lester Flatt's, then on around the lake past Roy Orbison's house. Then, down by a cove of the lake, was the most unusual home I'd ever seen. I stopped my car, got out and walked down to the cove and sat down on the bank and looked at the 200-foot-long thing under construction on the other side.

There were two big 35-foot round rooms, one on top of the other, on each end of the house. The center part, one room 130 feet long, had a large kitchen and bathroom. The whole house was being built on a solid strata of rock.

"A home with a strong foundation," I thought. "It might be the beginning of the rebuilding of my life — it might keep me with God as my life's foundation."

A wiry, suntanned man who was working at the house had noticed me and was walking over to me. "I'm Braxton Dixon," he said. "Can I help you?"

"Yes," I said. "Who can I buy that house from?"

"It isn't for sale," he laughed. "Everybody and his brother has tried to buy it, but I'm building it for myself."

"No, it's going to be mine," I said. "How much?"

"Are you Johnny Cash?" he asked.

"Yes," I said, "and I'm not kidding. That's going to be my home."

Braxton sat down and we talked and talked. "It's just that from the minute I saw it, I knew it was where I'd live," I told him.

He was awfully proud of the place. He explained how he had gone all over Tennessee and Kentucky buying up old barn timbers, hand-cut logs a hundred years old or more to use in the construction. The house was set against the side of the hill and followed the contour of the land. His "nature house" Braxton called it.

"But I can't sell it," he said. "My wife and son and I have put our hearts in this one, and we're gonna live here." He showed me through the house, and I felt like I'd come home when I walked in the front door.

"I don't blame you for wanting to keep it," I told him. "But a few things have come along in my life that I knew were meant to be, and I know I was meant to live in this house."

Ezra J. (Pop) Carter,

This book is dedicated to
Ezra J. Carter
who taught me to love the Word.

Cash home in Dyess, Arkansas

Johnny (J.R.) Cash, age 10

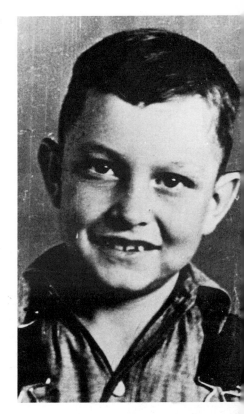

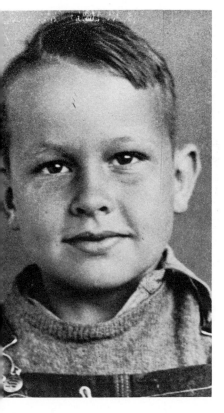

Jack Cash, age 12

Johnny at 18 —
senior class picture

Johnny about the time the
"High Noon Roundup"
came to Dyess.

**Staff Sergeant John R. Cash,
USAF in Germany, 1954**

**Buck Sergeant
John R. Cash**

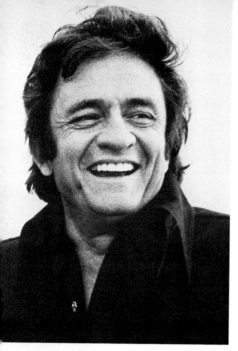

Johnny, 1974

Johnny and June Carter meet backstage at the Grand Ole Opry, July 1956

It's a boy! John Carter Cash, born March 3, 1970

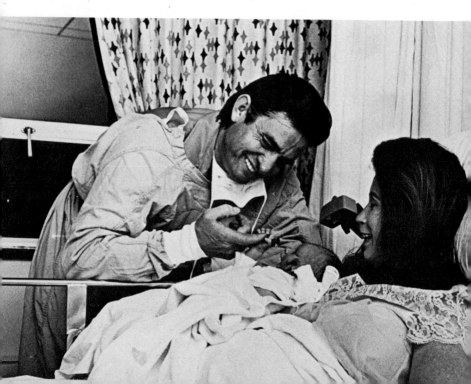

Carlene Smith Ruth,
June's daughter

Rosey Nix,
June's daughter

Rosanne Cash,
John's daughter

Cindy Cash,
John's daughter

Tara Cash,
John's daughter

Kathy Coggins,
John's daughter

John Carter listens to the playback at a record session.
— Photo by Jim Marshall, used by permission.

John, June, and Billy Graham

Mr. and Mrs. Ray Cash (seated) celebrate their 50th wedding anniversary with their children. Left to right: Roy, Louise, Johnny, Reba, Joann, Tommy

The Cash home on the lake.
Friends gather at the Cash home for an evening of fun.
— Photo by Jim Marshall, used by permission.

The Statler Brothers

John and the Tennessee Two, 1955. Left to right:
Luther Perkins, John, Marshall Grant

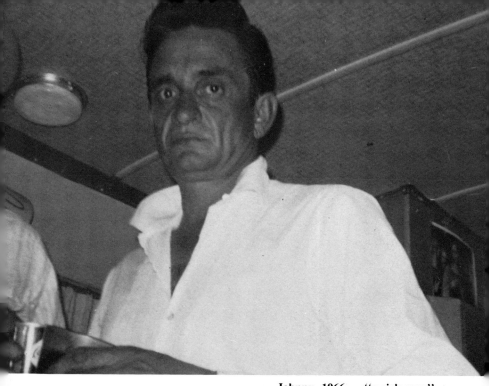

Johnny, 1966 — "a sick man"

1964

Marshall Grant,
bass

Bob Wootton,
lead guitar

Gordon Terry,
on the fiddle

W. S. Holland,
drummer

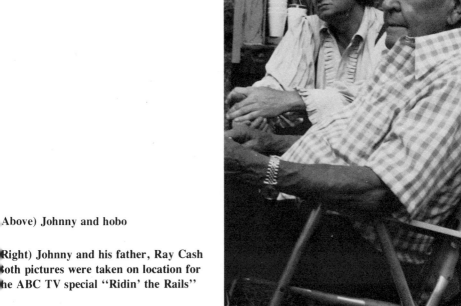

(Above) Johnny and hobo

(Right) Johnny and his father, Ray Cash
Both pictures were taken on location for
the ABC TV special "Ridin' the Rails"

1973

A visit to Dyess, 1969

Johnny, June and Carl Perkins in Saigon, Vietnam, 1969

Johnny and Sam Phillips (Sun Records), 1972

Left to right: Rev. Jimmy Snow, Rev. Floyd Gressett, Ray Cash, and Johnny, Las Vegas, 1971 — Photo by J. T. Phillips

Glen Sherley at Cash home, 1974 — Photo by Jim Marshall, used by permission.

The Carter Family
Left to right: Anita Carter Wootton, Maybelle Carter, Helen Carter Jones

John Carter Cash
Photo by Stephen Sparks

Johnny, 1974 — "a happy man"

(Left) Ray Cash (on location in
Georgia for "Ridin the Rails)

(Top) Johnny, Saul Holiff, and June
at CMA Awards Show, 1974 —
Photo by Jim Marshall, used by permiss

(Right) First public showing of
"Gospel Road," Nashville, 1972

The house had a rugged beauty with open rafters, the rough poplar barn boards and timbers, and the long wall of native limestone. There wasn't much I could tear up here, and there was plenty of room to walk the floor, which I would do for quite awhile yet.

Soon after I'd bought my house, Carl Perkins and W. S. Holland had come to visit me for a couple of days. I had called them and asked them to come.

"I think I can straighten up if the two of you will stay with me and give me encouragement for a few days," I told them over the phone.

W. S. said, "If you really mean that, we'll move in with you for as long as you like."

"I really mean it," I said.

By the time they got there, I was high, and Carl started drinking to be able to stand me.

"Let's go for a ride in my jeep," I said.

"If you'll let me drive," W. S. said. "Let's face it. I'm the only sober one here."

"No, I will," and I got behind the wheel.

Then I gave them the scariest ride of their lives. I turned the jeep into the woods, got off the road and made a new one. Up hills and down, through fences, crashing through gates, chasing the cattle that were grazing in neighboring fields. W. S. turned pale and held onto his seat. Carl kept drinking. Finally I turned back into my driveway, and we got out.

"For the first time in my life, I thought about taking a drink," W. S. said.

"Come on in and I'll cook us something to eat," I said. I started cutting up a ham to fry. I made biscuits and gravy and scrambled eggs. The kitchen looked like a disaster area, but Carl and W. S. ate a big meal. I, of course, wasn't hungry.

As they finished eating, Carl said, "Well, John, I'll

tell you what. I'm in no shape to help you, even if you wanted me to. I'm going home."

W. S. said, "Well — I hate to go because I'd stay till Christmas if it would help. But you're not ready yet, are you, John?"

I sobered a little. "I guess not," I said. "I thought I was, but I guess not."

"Call me when I can help, and I'll be here," said W. S. And they were gone.

May 20, 1967, was the twenty-third anniversary of my brother Jack's death. To commemorate it, the pills prompted me to do a strange thing.

I'd just bought the house from Braxton Dixon out on the lake and had one room furnished plus the kitchen. I was living in the "bachelor apartment" in the house. I decided I would fly my mother and daddy in from California and get my brother Roy and sister Louise to come in from Memphis, my sister Joanne from Houston, and my brother Tommy from Nashville. My plan was to have a big dinner at the house on the anniversary of Jack's death.

Reba called them all for me, and at first nobody said they'd come. I'm sure they all thought I wasn't serious, coming up with such a suggestion. I asked Reba to impress upon the family the importance of the "reunion" to me. She talked to them all again, and they agreed to be there.

My mother and daddy didn't want to come back alone, so I flew to California to get them and bring them back to Tennessee. But when I got to California, I got a supply of pills to take back to Nashville. I'd been up for about three days and nights straight with no sleep, and I was told later (I don't remember) that when we landed in Memphis I got up out of my seat, passed out, and fell on my face on the floor of the plane. I had taken barbiturates, thinking I would sleep until Memphis, but evidently I had taken far too many.

The pilot told mother and daddy, "You'll have to get him out of here. He can't fly on to Nashville on this plane." They had me carried off, called Roy who hadn't yet left Memphis, and took me to a motel.

The next thing I remember was the following day on the plane going into Nashville. I stumbled and staggered off the plane, still groggy from barbiturates. My brother Tommy met us at the gate, and he was very angry. "Don't you care what you're doing to mamma and daddy?" he cried.

I yelled something back, and he took a swing at me. I remember swinging back, then a scuffle, and somebody stopped the fight. I was cursing Tommy and calling him names. He looked at me with tears in his eyes, shook his head, and walked away.

Five minutes later I had completely forgotten that anything had happened; I had not the least bit of personal concern over the incident. I didn't know anybody in the Nashville airport had even seen the scuffle happen, nor did I suspect anybody in Memphis had seen me being carried off that plane, or that anybody aboard had seen me fall on my face the day before. Something whispered to me, "Nobody saw you, Cash. Nobody heard you. Don't worry about it."

We arrived at the house on the lake, and I didn't even have a chair there for my folks to sit on. Here I had brought them in from California, and there was no place for them even to sleep.

There was a big round bed upstairs, and I had taken it over, but I finally realized that mother and daddy had to have a bed. I found a quilt and put it down behind the fireplace — not that I intended to sleep, because I didn't — and they slept in my bed upstairs.

The next day, May 20, Roy and my sister Louise were the first to arrive. Tommy forgave me and came on out to the house, Reba flew in from California, and Joanne came up from Houston.

We were all sitting around visiting that morning, when it suddenly dawned on me I'd invited them back for a *dinner* that day. Not only was there no food, there was no one to cook it or serve it. So I called June Carter and told her my problem. She couldn't believe what was happening, but she came on out to help.

That was a bad scene, too. She came out and tried to prepare a meal. I argued with her about what she was cooking or wasn't cooking. The table wasn't perfect. This or that wasn't cooked for the dinner. "I want everything just so for this special occasion," I said. She walked out crying once and started home, but turned around and came back and miraculously prepared the evening meal.

I hired a photographer to come out and take pictures of the whole family around the table. As best as I can remember, everyone went along with everything I'd arranged without question. Much later I'd realize just how much love and long-suffering my parents had for me.

I think in some of my weird, wild imaginings that the little boy in me had called mama and daddy and all the brothers and sisters to come back home on May 20 to witness what I was possibly thinking in my drugged mind — Jack was going to come back and sit down at the table with us. Though I knew better — I didn't really believe it — the drug demons kept promoting the idea.

Even though I had learned well the ways and tricks of Deception, it is only recently I have realized the eerie "spiritual" significance of that anniversary incident.

I had a vacant chair at the table where Jack would sit. When Jack did not appear, Satan probably figured that in my shame and disappointment I might reject the idea of the second appearance of Christ also. What a genius Satan is at imitation. He knew that I believed in Christ. And since Jack didn't show up, maybe I would believe Jesus wouldn't come again, either.

Everyone went to bed afterwards except me. I roamed around the place for hours. Then, I got in my car and went after some beer, but stayed out all night. When I came in about daylight, I took a handful of barbiturates and lay down on the floor behind the fireplace.

I tossed and turned for a long, long time, and I heard daddy and mother walking around the room upstairs. I suppose they thought I was finally asleep.

"I wish he just had a chair for us to sit down on," I heard daddy say.

Roy walked into the room, and mama asked him, "Roy, do you think John's going to be all right?" There was a resignation in her voice indicating that my life was in God's hands now. It was up to Him if I lived or died.

"He'll be OK, mama," Roy said. "He's been through the fire for a special reason. I don't know what the reason is, but he'll be OK."

Mama sounded reassured. "I've always said that God had His hand on John, and He still does."

When I woke up, I was all alone again. Everybody was gone. My brother Roy told me later that he never expected to see me alive again.

June Carter came back the next day, brought me something to eat, and cleaned up the house.

11 / Seven One-Night Stands

I had to get a work permit to perform at the Hilton Hotel in Las Vegas. It doesn't matter if you're a guitar player or what, everybody has to have one. So during our first booking at the Hilton in 1971 they came backstage with these personal information forms. There were several specific questions to answer, and then at the bottom of the page were five spaces — if you needed that many — where it said, "Have you ever been arrested? Where? When? For what?"

I didn't know until I started writing that five spaces wouldn't be enough. I had to turn the paper over and put some answers on the back. Because for the first time I realized it was seven times I'd been in jail. Seven different times, seven different places. And for five of the seven I couldn't tell them what I had been busted for; I never did really know.

The seven arrests were over a seven-year period. Seven steps down, an average of once a year. Filling out that form backstage at the Hilton, I began to reflect on those episodes.

There was that time in Nashville in 1959, which was the first time I was in jail. I know what that one was for — public drunkenness, and I deserved to be in jail. I was trying to break down a door and get in a club that had already closed.

Another time, I was out after our concert drinking beer in Starkville, Mississippi. It was reported that when they stopped me I was picking flowers in someone's yard at 2:00 A.M. Actually I was walking down the sidewalk trying to find a service station open where I could buy some cigarettes. The police picked me up and took me to jail. I went into a rage — screaming, cussing, and kicking at the cell door all night long until I finally broke my big toe. At 8:00 the next morning they let me out when they knew I was sober.

Other times I was in overnight in Nevada, Texas, and California. The police found me wandering around on pills and alcohol and put me in jail with the rest of the drunks till I slept it off.

There were some hairy experiences in those jails. Like the big, burly lumberjack in Carson City, Nevada, who sat on the bunk opposite mine, crying. His mood would keep changing. He'd get angry, and he'd stand up and pound his chest and yell like Tarzan. He'd show me his powerful arms and tell me he could break my neck like a twig. And I knew he could.

I did some fast talking, complimenting his muscles, saying, "I know you can! I know you can!" I was very sober by then. An arm the size of a mule's leg went around my neck, and I started singing. He stopped for a moment. I sang *Folsom Prison Blues* and *I Walk the Line,* and he sat down, trying to figure me out.

Finally he said, "You sound like Johnny Cash."

With a sigh of relief, I said, "I *am* Johnny Cash."

And that made him angry. "You're a liar," he said, and he stood up to challenge my remark.

Now I was not only sober, but really praying.

"Sing," he commanded.

I sang one of the songs I had recorded in an album of hymns, during some of my better days, *When He Reached Down His Hand for Me*.

When He reached down His hand for me,
When He reached down for me,
I was lost and undone
Without my God or His Son,
When He reached down His hand for me.

The big lumberjack had tears in his eyes now. "Sing another one," he said, and I sang another one. After that one he said, crying, "Me and you are a couple of drunks, but you sure sound like Johnny Cash. Sing another one."

He laid down and closed his eyes, and I sang until I knew he was asleep. Soon it was morning and they let me go.

By 1965, I was taking more pills than I could find doctors to supply. In Nashville, as in California, I easily found illegal sources; a friend, for example, would know someone who worked in a drugstore. That friend would get me hundreds of pills at a time through altering order blanks from distributors. Or, in a couple of instances, I was supplied through drugstores where, because of large demand for pills from people like me, large quantities were brought in illegally from Mexico or from fly-by-night manufacturers.

On a stopover from Dallas to L.A., I decided to cross the border myself at El Paso to obtain a supply. I had run out of pills or had lost those I had, so I hired a cab and asked the driver to get me all he could.

I was nervous and a little afraid as I sat waiting a short time later in Juarez while the driver got out of the car and went into a bar to get the amphetamines and barbiturates. I felt like the outlaw I had become, sitting in

a taxicab on a hot, dirty back street behind a bar in Mexico
waiting impatiently for the pusher to fill my order. I slid
down a little lower in the back seat each time someone
looked my way. I had never done it this way before, but
I'd been told by a pill-head in Nashville I could get
all I wanted in Mexico.

He was right. The taxi driver soon returned with
several hundred of both kinds of pills, and we headed back
across the border and to my hotel in El Paso.

When I got back to the room, I popped three or
four and soon started rambling. I ended up in downtown
El Paso where I bought an antique pistol in a pawn shop. It
was a nineteenth-century cap and ball type and was in
perfect working order.

As I walked out of the shop, a man stopped me.
I found out later he'd been following me since I'd come
back across the border.

"Hello, Johnny Cash. I'm a fan of yours," said
the plainclothesman.

I knew instantly he was a policeman, though it did
not occur to me that he knew of my trip across the line
into Mexico. I assumed he was watching me because of
the gun.

"I collect antique pistols," I said, showing him
the relic.

"It's a nice one," he said in a friendly manner.
"Do you have a show in El Paso?"

"No — just passing through on my way to L.A."
I answered, turning to walk away.

"I've got all your records," he said, walking
beside me.

"Thank you," I said. Does he know I'm on the
pills, I wondered.

"When are you leaving El Paso?" he asked.

"Tonight at 9:00," I said. And I got in a cab and
returned to the hotel.

I tied up the pills in two socks and put one of them inside my guitar and the other in the lining of my suitcase. A little wariness came over me about leaving at 9:00 since I had announced my departure time to that policeman.

But the gun was legal — an antique. Besides, he'd seen it. The pills? They were well-hidden — except for the dozen or so I had in my pocket.

I reached the airport a bit early and checked my suitcase and guitar in at the ticket counter. I got on board the plane as soon as they would let me and took my seat with my briefcase containing the pistol on my lap.

The plane door was about to be closed when I heard a man tell the stewardess, "Wait a minute — we've got to take a man off here."

"Who?" she asked.

"Johnny Cash," the voice said. "Where's he sitting?"

He stepped inside, and I recognized him immediately as the man I'd seen and talked with outside the pawn shop.

"I'm right here," I said quietly, embarrassed. "What do you want?"

"Do you have a gun?" he asked.

By now, everyone one the plane was watching and listening. He was sweating, nervous, out of breath, as if he'd been running.

"You know I do," I answered. "I showed it to you this afternoon. What about it?"

"Come on, let's go," said another man who had just appeared in sight. By now I was glad to get off the plane and away from all those passengers who had witnessed my arrest.

They took me inside the terminal to an empty room. Empty, except for my guitar and suitcase. That was what the rush had been about. They had barely managed to get my bags and me off the plane before it took off.

They shook me down, found the pills in my pocket, opened my suitcase and began a systematic search of every piece of clothing in it. Then, they found the pills in the lining.

"Do you have any more?" one of them asked.

"No," I said.

He opened the guitar case, removed the guitar and shook it.

"Do you want to loosen the strings so you can get them out, or do you want us to break the guitar to get them?"

I didn't answer. I took the guitar, loosened the strings, reached my hand inside and brought out the rest of the pills.

They poured them all out in a big ashtray and looked at them. They examined the guitar case again, and then both men sat down and looked at me.

"Where is the H?" one asked.

"The what?" I said.

"The H, the horse, the heroin?" he demanded.

I had been calm, quiet, and submissive to their search and seizure up to this time, but now I saw their real reason for it and became angry.

"Is that why you arrested me? Because you thought I had heroin?" I asked.

They didn't reply.

"I don't have heroin," I said. "I've never touched heroin."

"What are you on?" one asked.

"Dexedrine," I answered. "You've got it all there in the ashtray."

After a moment one of them looked at the other and asked, as if I weren't even there, "Do you believe him?"

"I think I do," came the response.

"You see, Cash," one of them continued, "we apprehended you because your cab driver made your purchase from a known heroin pusher. We thought sure the contact was for heroin."

I began to breathe easier, thinking maybe they weren't going to hold me.

"These are amphetamines and barbiturates," I said. "You can get them from most any doctor on prescription. I just wanted enough to last me for awhile."

"But you got them illegally," they said. "We'll have to book you."

My cell in the El Paso jail hadn't been cleaned since its last occupant. The plumbing didn't work. There was no mattress, no pillow — just a dirty blanket over the springs.

The light stayed on all night. I watched the roaches crawl across the floor. Some of the other inmates were laughing and cursing each other. I heard a boy crying and another one praying. I tried to pray and couldn't.

The pills wore off about sunup, and I finally slept. At noon they brought me a bowl of black-eyed peas and a piece of bread, which I ate.

"You have a phone call," said the man with the keys who unlocked my cell door.

"Who is it?" I asked.

"How do I know?" he said. "Come on."

"John, this is Sam," said the voice on the other end. "Is there anything I can do?"

"Sam who?" I asked, trembling.

"Sam Phillips," he said. "What do you want me to do? Should I come down there? Can I send my lawyer? What can I do?"

I wanted to ask him how he'd found out, but I was afraid he'd tell me he'd heard it on the news. I hadn't seen Sam in two years, and at a time when I figured nobody cared much for me, here he was on the phone.

"I'll be all right. Thank you anyway."

I choked up and couldn't say anything else, so I hung up.

Back in the cell a few minutes later, the same man returned. "You have a phone call, Cash," he said.

It was Neal Merritt, songwriter and disc jockey on El Paso's country music station.

"Sorry to hear about your trouble, John," he said. "Can I do anything?"

"How did you hear about it, Neal?" I asked.

"It came over the Teletype," he answered.

"Oh, no," I said. "My mother, father, my wife, my children — they all know about it by now."

I didn't think I'd have the strength to make it back to the cell. Then another call. This time it was Don Law, my record producer at the time from Columbia. How many times I had failed to show up at recording sessions because I knew I wouldn't be able to sing. How many times Don had sat at the control booth all night long, hoping I'd get in the mood to cut a record. And he'd never complained, never criticized. He even turned his apartment over to me at times when I was unable to face the world. Now here he was, on the phone with me, encouraging me, telling me he'd help.

I was numb when I hung up. "I don't want any more calls," I told the man with the keys as I walked on wobbling legs back to my cell. And fell down on the bunk.

"I don't ever want out of this cell again," I said silently to myself. "I just want to stay here alone and pray that God will forgive me and then let me die. Because I'm too weak to face everyone I'll have to face. Knowing my family is heartbroken, knowing my friends and fans are hurt and disappointed — it's more than I can reconcile with them."

I could see my family crying. I could hear them ask, "Why, daddy?" "Why, John?" "Why, son?"

And I cried. I wanted to pray, but I could only cry.

"You have a phone call, Cash," the man said again.

"Leave me alone," I said. And he left.

A few minutes later he was back, opening the door, tapping me on the shoulder.

"Come on," he said.

At the front desk, a lawyer, Woodrow Bean, and two policemen stood waiting.

"Marshall Grant called me," said the lawyer. "Know him?"

"Yes," I said.

"Bond is being posted, and we have to go over to the courthouse to get you released," he stated. "Put on these sunglasses."

"Why?" I asked.

"Because you have to wear *these*," said one of the policemen, as he put handcuffs on me. "Sorry, but it's the law."

"This will soon be over with, Mr. Cash," said Lawyer Bean. "When we go out the door, stay right with me and walk fast."

"Why?" I asked again. By now I was dazed, scared, ashamed. *Handcuffed.* How could I drop so low?

"Because," said Mr. Bean, "there are several press photographers waiting for you to come outside."

The pictures in the newspapers across the country the next morning, including the Memphis *Press-Scimitar,* were a public documentation of the low point of my entire career. I faced the shame from it sober for the next six weeks. But as humbling and defacing as it all was, the memory of embarrassment faded into the heightening schedule of demanding tours. And I returned once again to my shadows of death — the pills.

My last time in jail was one night in October 1967 at Lafayette, Georgia. And that was the turning point of it all.

The following morning at 8:00 Sheriff Ralph Jones came in and wakened me. I got up with that old familiar sick, sober, and sorry feeling.

He said, "Come on up to the desk, Mr. Cash."

I walked up to his desk and stood there waiting to

be reprimanded and admonished like they usually did. Sheriff Jones opened up a drawer in his desk and took out my money and a handful of pills. He held them in his hand and looked up at me and said, "I'm going to give you your money and your dope back because you know better than most people that God gave you a free will to do with yourself whatever you want to do. Here's your money and your pills. Now you can throw the pills away or you can take them and go ahead and kill yourself. Whichever one you want to do, Mr. Cash, will be all right with me."

I stood looking at him a long time before I could answer.

"But I don't understand why you're giving me the dope back. It's illegal."

He said, "Right, it's illegal. It would be a sin and a crime for you to kill yourself, too. And that's exactly what those pills are doing to you.

"I've followed your career for over ten years," he continued. "My wife and I have every record you've ever made. We love you. We've always loved you. We've watched for you on television, listened for you on the radio. We've got your albums of hymns. We're probably the best two fans you've ever had.

"It broke my heart when they brought you in here last night. I left the jail and went home to my wife and told her I had Johnny Cash locked up. I almost wanted to resign and just walk out because it was such a heartbreaking thing for me."

And he slapped the pills down on the desk and said, "Go on. Take 'em and get out of here."

And I picked them up and said, "Sheriff, you won't be sorry that you let me go like this."

He said, "Do with your life whatever you want to. Just remember, you've got the free will to either kill yourself or save your life."

I put the money in my pocket and walked out of jail. Just three or four dollars was all I had left. I threw the pills on the ground. A friend of mine, Richard McGibony, was waiting in his car. He'd found out I'd been picked up and had come there to wait, hoping they'd let me out the next morning.

I got in the car and said, "Richard, I'm going back home to Nashville. You'll never see me high on dope any more."

"I hope you mean it," he replied.

"That sheriff back there is something else," I said. "God sent him to me, or sent me to him. He made me know, he made me realize I really was about to kill myself. He also made me remember that I really can live."

So I went back home to Nashville, and I called June.

"I'm home," I said.

"How are you John?" she asked.

"I'm all right. But I wish you would call (Dr.) Nat Winston (who was then Tennessee Commissioner of Mental Health) and see if he can come out and talk to me, because I need help. See if he can give me some pointers on how to fight the terrors from the devil who's busy crawling up my back."

She called back later and said, "Nat is gone all day long everyday, way into the night. But he said if you will see him, he'll be out tomorrow night when he gets in from East Tennessee."

I made it through the night. But the next day I found a bottle of amphetamines I had hidden in the bathroom. And having been off them only two days, I swallowed a handful.

I don't remember what I did the rest of the day. But just about dark, I decided to get my tractor out of the shed and drive along the cliff overlooking the lake to see how close I could get to the edge without going over. It was then late October and already very cold. I had on a long leather topcoat and the rest of the pills in my pocket.

The tractor moved along the edge of the cliff overlooking the lake. Suddenly the earth gave way underneath me. The next thing I knew I hit the lake, the tractor coming down from above. It turned over and barely missed me.

I tried to crawl up out of the ice-cold water onto the bank, but I was stiff from the cold. A moment later, almost from out of nowhere, Braxton Dixon came running down to the water and reached out his hand to me. Right behind him were June and Nat Winston.

I was so cold I couldn't talk, and they took me in the house. I didn't want them to get my coat because I knew the rest of the pills were in that pocket. But they managed to get the coat off and away from me, and they found the pills and got rid of them. I went to bed and finally went to sleep from exhaustion.

About four in the morning I woke up, and sitting in the chair beside my bed was Nat. I really didn't know him too well at that time.

He said, "How are you feeling, John?"

I sat up immediately, thinking about my pills, trying to remember where I'd put them, and said, "Oh, great, great, Nat. I feel great." ("If I could just have a few pills to kind of taper off on," I thought.)

"You look hellish," he said.

That put my head back down on the pillow, because I knew from then on there'd be no fooling Nat Winston. I knew if I tried to slip a pill with Nat around, it would never work.

He said, "I wanted to be sure and be here when you woke up. When you called me, I figured you wouldn't have done it if you hadn't really intended to get your life straightened out."

"I never meant anything more sincerely," I said. "But I see I need some advice on how to fight the problem from somebody like you."

"John," Nat said, "I'm a doctor, I'm a psychiatrist, and I've seen a lot of people in the shape you're in. And frankly, I don't think there is much chance for you. I've never known of anyone as far gone as you are to really whip it. Only you can do it, and it would be a lot easier if you let God help you."

I knew he was right. God had been waiting all this time for me to come back. Now that He knew I was finally serious, He was beginning to surround me with His people to fight with me — Nat Winston, June, her parents, my parents, Braxton Dixon, and others. But mainly it was my fight. Only I could do it, and I had to lean on God — like He knew I'd have to.

"I'll do it, Nat," I said.

"Get set for the fight of your life," he said. "I'll be back tomorrow night, and we'll see how you're doing."

He left me alone, and I faced the truth that I had long known: there could be no tapering off; I had to get off them — or die. One pill would call for another, and another, and. . . .

There would be no fooling anyone. Especially myself.

12 / Splinters, Briars, and Worms

Nat Winston told June, "If Johnny Cash is going to live, somebody must move out there with him and keep the wrong crowd out."

She talked with her father about it the next day.

"Well, what are you waiting on?" E. J. Carter said. "Pack your suitcase and Maybelle and I will go, too."

June, Maybelle, and E. J. Carter moved out to my house and slept in sleeping bags down on the lower floor. As Nat Winston predicted, they needed to be there because I couldn't have stayed alone at the time, and their being there encouraged me. Braxton Dixon's wife, Anna, volunteered to sit up all night one night and make sure no one bothered me.

I never knew who the people were who tried to see me, and I never asked. But I knew I had not only a habit to fight, but a life style to change. I locked myself in my bedroom. I saw nobody. This was going to be my "forty days in the wilderness."

One night a persistent friend of mine tried to force his way in to get upstairs to see me. Anna Dixon told him, "No." When he persisted, she stopped him just inside the door with a butcher knife in her hand, and she backed him all the way to the car with the knife at his throat. She never told me who he was, just that he said he was my friend. But he was high on something and rude, until she came up with the knife.

Nat came by everyday. Sometimes it was five o'clock in the afternoon and other times it was midnight, but he didn't miss for thirty days. Everyday I had his personal visits and his counsel to look forward to, and it gave me courage to fight.

If people actually knew the terrors of coming off drugs — understand, I was what people like to call "habituated" to amphetamines and barbiturates. That sounds nicer than "addicted." I sometimes took as many as twenty a day of five and ten-milligram amphetamines. It took that many barbiturates, Equanil or meprobamate, a few at a time over two or three hours, to bring me down enough to doze off and get a little sleep. Then six or eight more amphetamines the next day to get me going. The amphetamines were tough to kick, but the barbiturates were what caused the real terror.

My third night home, the first night June's parents were there, I made it fairly well. June and her family prayed for me. I didn't go to sleep for a long time, though I did sleep finally.

I woke up feeling bad the next day, craving something to get me going. The whole day was terrible. I was nervous, I was sweating, but I never left my room upstairs. When it came time to go to bed that night, I was walking the floor and climbing the walls, wanting something to calm me down.

I didn't have the peace inside for a lot of praying, but every breath was a prayer, a fighting prayer, and I wasn't giving up. I had turned it over to God. I had humbled myself. I was asking Him to help.

That night when I went to bed, I finally got to sleep about two or three o'clock in the morning. And that was when the nightmares started coming. They came every night for about ten nights.

It was the same nightmare every night, and it affected my stomach — I suppose because the stomach was where the pills had landed, exploded, and done their work. I'd be lying in bed on my back or curled up on my side. The cramps would come and go, and I'd roll over, doze off, and go to sleep.

Then all of a sudden a glass ball would begin to expand in my stomach. My eyes were closed, but I could see it. It would grow to the size of a baseball, a volleyball, then a basketball. And about the time I felt that ball was twice the size of a basketball, it lifted me up off the bed.

I was in a strange state of half-asleep and half-awake. I couldn't open my eyes, and I couldn't close them. It lifted me off the bed to the ceiling, and when it would go through the roof, the glass ball would explode and tiny, infinitesimal slivers of glass would go out into my bloodstream from my stomach. I could feel the pieces of glass being pumped through my heart into the veins of my arms, my legs, my feet, my neck, and my brain, and some of them would come out the pores of my skin. Then I'd float back down through the ceiling onto my bed and wake up. I'd turn over on my side for awhile, unable to sleep. Then I'd lie on my back, doze off, get almost asleep — and the same nightmare would come again.

I never imagined a hole in the roof. I just went right through it without an opening. Sometimes in addition to glass coming out of my skin and the corners of my eyes, I would be pulling splinters of wood and briars and thorns out of my flesh, and sometimes worms. I wanted to scream, but I couldn't.

The Carters and Dixons brought me food, but I

rarely ate. Temptation didn't give up, and I turned my room upside-down — the door locked tight — looking for pills. I looked in shoes. I looked in pockets of clothes in the closet. I knew they were there somewhere, but I couldn't find them.

Sometimes in the midst of those nightmares, I'd get up and start jerking drawers out of dressers. I'd turn the bed over, tear up the bathroom. I'd pull up the carpet, pull down the curtains, feel around the windows, tear down the cornices. I did everything looking for pills I might have hidden over the past two or three years.

But I didn't find any.

When I had been asleep my first night home, June and Nat found every pill in the room. I discovered later that they gathered about a quart jar full. If they hadn't, I would never have made it.

I told June after a few days, "Don't give up. I'm going to win."

She assured me she believed it this time. "Call on God, John. Don't weaken."

"I already weakened, but I didn't find any. You found them, didn't you?"

"Yes," she said. "Are you sorry?"

"No," I said. "Thank God you did. I'm a little stronger. It's downhill so far as this fight is concerned, but I have a feeling that every day is going to be a brand-new mountain."

"I'll climb them with you," she said. "God will pull us to the top." June was finally winning her part of the fight, and I was sharing in the victory.

At the end of three weeks and through my talks with Nat, I was gaining confidence and strength. I was able to sleep again. I was still careful and wary, and I knew June was, but after four weeks off the pills, everyone really started to believe I was going to make it. I began praying in earnest and thanking Him for a new life, for I felt like a new person.

Word got around. Pill heads and pushers stopped coming; so did the people with whom I'd been taking drugs.

There were those in the music business who had written me off as hopeless. There were those who had lost confidence in me and wouldn't buy any news about me reforming or changing for the better because they had heard it all before from time to time.

Those close to me, the Statler Brothers, the Carter Family, Luther Perkins, Marshall Grant, and W. S. Holland, thrilled at the change in me. It was going to be hard for them to forget the old Johnny Cash because they had known him a long time, but they all called, congratulating me and sharing the joy in the good news.

June testified to them that God had given me back my life. They understood that and they were proud for me, but it would take some time to prove that it was for good this time, and I knew I had to prove myself to everyone — especially me.

November 11, 1967, I was asked to perform a benefit concert for the Hendersonville High School to raise money for band uniforms to send our hometown kids to the Orange Bowl in Miami. I'd volunteered to do it back in the summer. By the time the show came up, I'd been off the pills four weeks and felt like I'd be able to do it.

The Sunday before the concert June called and asked if I felt like going to church.

"I don't know if I'm ready to face the world," I said.

"We'll just slip in the back after the service starts," she said.

"I'll drive," I said, when we walked out to her car. It was the first time I'd driven in a month. We drove to the Baptist church in Hendersonville.

June started kidding me. "Look how good you're driving," she said when we were about halfway there. "You're not weaving and jerking like you used to. I'm not even having to hold on to the dashboard."

"I think you're going to like me when you get to know me," I said. "I'm even beginning to like myself again."

Courtney Wilson, the pastor, preached a sermon called "Jesus, the Living Water." He talked about the spiritual drought men put themselves through. How men destroy themselves in a worldly desert, living a life that is arid and fruitless, going down to death, when all the time God pleads for us to drink of Jesus, the living water, the water of life. I hung on every word of his sermon, and I wondered as I sat there if Rev. Wilson knew he was preaching directly to me.

Afterwards, I took June to lunch, and we talked about the concert coming up at the high school. "Not only do I not dread it," I said, "I think I'm going to enjoy it."

"It will be the first one you've done without pills for a long time, won't it, John?" June asked.

"Yes, it will," I said. "I can't remember how long ago I did a show without them."

"It will be even harder," she said, "doing your first one here in your hometown."

"I'll make it," I said. "I'm going to drink of that living water that Courtney Wilson talked about."

I went onstage that evening with the worst case of butterflies I'd ever known. But I prayed, and I smiled, and I sang.

After two or three songs, I gained more confidence. Then I opened up. I laughed, I joked, and I talked between songs. I sang for an hour, and I could never remember feeling so strong and sure of myself as I did that night.

I gave the audience no indication of the apprehension I'd felt a few days before or of the butterflies at the beginning. June was crying tears of joy. I could see her standing backstage, grinning at me, and I gave her the "thumbs up," "everything is all right" signal.

We closed the show with *Were You There When They Crucified My Lord?* and I felt about six feet off the floor. I felt Him with me. I was more alive than I'd ever been before. I knew I was again holding onto the Man I was singing about in that song, and I knew He was still holding me.

> Were you there when they crucified my Lord?
> Were you there when they crucified my Lord?
> Oh! Sometimes it causes me to tremble,
>   tremble, tremble,
> Were you there when they crucified my Lord?
>
> Were you there when they nailed Him to the
>   tree?
> Were you there when they nailed Him to the
>   tree?
> Oh! Sometimes it causes me to tremble,
>   tremble, tremble,
> Were you there when they nailed Him to the
>   tree?

13 / **Prisoner's Song**

Carl Perkins had become a regular member of my show in 1967. I hadn't seen him much in the past ten years, but I'd heard a lot about him.

He and I realized that our lives had another parallel besides our childhood and music. He had become a heavy drinker and for the past seven years had considered himself an alcoholic. He never did a concert that he didn't consume at least a fifth of whiskey, but I never noticed that it affected his performing. I was proud to have an old friend working with me, especially if we had a common vice.

Carl rarely took pills, but in many ways amphetamines and alcohol are alike in the hold they take on you. The more Carl drank, the more he cried and talked about God. I did likewise when on the pills for a long time. With the loosening of the tongue through our false stimulants we had many long talks, crying on each other's shoulders about how rotten we were.

When that high school benefit came up at Hendersonville months later, Carl was sober and pale. He'd heard I had been straight for a month. Though he and everybody else on the show were "waiting to see," he

knew I'd been clean four weeks and that if he drank he'd be
the only one on the show doing so. Nobody else drank
at all or had the pill habit I did.

Carl said little to me that night — just watched me
carefully, seeing for himself if it were true or not. After
the show he was gone, and when he joined me two weeks
later on tour in California, he was drunk.

In San Diego Carl had a good performance, but
proceeded to get drunk afterwards. He avoided all of us,
and we didn't see him until time to leave the next day — and
he had the hangover of his life when he boarded our bus.
He lay on the bunk moaning and crying while we headed up
the coast.

We stopped on the beach at Ventura to have a
picnic and heard Carl cry, "I'm dying."

June started talking to him. "Look at John, Carl,"
she said. "He was dying. Call on God. Turn it over to
Him and you'll live."

"I can't live," he cried. "I ought to die. God can't
love me any more.

"Oh yes He does," she said. "You talk to Him."

We walked off the bus and left him lying there on
the bed. After a few minutes I got back on the bus, and
Carl was standing up. He was still crying, and he had a bottle
of whiskey in his hand. Tears were streaming down his
cheeks.

"Are you still drinking, Carl?" I asked.

"No, John," he answered. "If I can walk off this
bus, I'm going to throw this bottle away."

"Come on, I'll help you," I said.

"No, I'm going to do it myself," Carl said. "If you
can do it, so can I. He's my God, too."

I moved out of his way, and Carl walked toward
the surf. June, Marshall, Luther, W. S., and I watched
him. He threw the bottle into the ocean, then dropped to his
knees. We could hear him saying, "God have mercy on
me," over and over and over.

He stayed there for a long time while we went on with our lunch. When he finally got up and walked toward us, he was a new man. A healing transformation had taken place in a matter of minutes.

"Have a sandwich, Carl," I said.

"No, thank you, John. Later. I think I'll go to sleep for awhile."

"You look better," said June.

"I am. I'm going to live," he said, tears again coming to his eyes. "I'm going to live!"

The healing power did a complete job in Carl Perkins. He has not had a drink since that day.

Most of Carl Perkins' talent has never been recognized. He has always been a fine ballad singer and writer, as well as being somewhat the originator of country-rock.

In addition to that, though, with his coming back to God in 1967 Carl wrote a song which I recorded the following year, as did dozens of gospel singers and groups afterwards. The song was about our lives as boys — mine and Carl's — and the love in our families and the family circle that would not be broken, for someday we'd sing around God's throne.

There was even a line in the song about my brother Jack: "Me and little brother will join right in there."

The song: *Daddy Sang Bass*.

> I remember when I was a lad,
> Times were hard and things were bad,
> But there's a silver lining behind every cloud.
> Just poor people that's all we were,
> Trying to make a living out of black land dirt,
> We'd get together in a family circle singing
>   loud.
>
> Daddy sang bass, mama sang tenor,
> Me and little brother would join right in there,
> 'Cause singin' seems to help a troubled soul.

One of these days, and it won't be long,
I'll rejoin them in a song,
I'm gonna join the family circle at the throne.

No, the circle won't be broken,
Bye and bye, Lord, bye and bye,
Daddy'll sing bass, mama'll sing tenor,
Me and little brother will join right in there,
In the sky, Lord, in the sky.

By Carl Perkins, © Cedarwood Publishing Co. Used by permission.

I had played my first prison concert back in the late fifties. The first appearance I made at a prison was at Huntsville, Texas State Prison, in 1957. Carl performed at many, many prisons with me in later years, as did the Statler Brothers and the Carter Family. I always felt it was one way of giving back to the American people some of the good they had given us.

And by doing a prison concert, we were letting inmates know that somewhere out there in the free world was somebody who cared for them as human beings. With fewer crimes in our land, on our streets, as our aim, maybe when those men were paroled back into society's mainstream, there'd be less hostility knowing someone had cared.

We've done thirty-five to forty prison concerts, and one short letter I received from an inmate at Nevada State Penitentiary following the appearance there was well worth the time, cost, and trouble of playing them all. I had told the men that day, "We're here for several reasons, in case you don't know why we're here. We're here because the inmate population petitioned us to come. We're here because we love the applause you give us in prison. And I'm here because I'm a Christian."

The letter from the inmate read: "Dear Johnny, I know now what Jesus meant when He said He was sent to the captives, because I saw Him in you today."

The applause and wild response was one way they were allowed to let off steam. They'd stomp their feet, bang the tables, yell, whistle, clap their hands, and make as much noise as they could because it was "allowed." I always thought it would be an exciting sound to get that applause on record.

Merle Haggard was an inmate at San Quentin Prison the first time we appeared there on January 1, 1958. I had been on a tour of one-nighters in California, playing mostly clubs and ballrooms. Gordon Terry was working with me on a regular basis, as he did for three or four years as a featured act on my show.

Johnny Western, writer and singer of *Ballad of Paladin* ("Have Gun, Will Travel"), acted as M. C. for my shows and sang a few songs. Gordon and Johnny were always excellent performers and showmen.

After Gordon had introduced me to pills, I introduced them to other people like Johnny Western and Luther Perkins. But none of the others around me ever went as far with the habit as I did.

Gordon Terry stayed on pills and alcohol much longer than I did. He eventually went off on his own, playing exclusively in clubs, bars, and honky-tonks. He traveled a long, long road toward self-destruction, until finally in 1974 he came to Christ at a Bob Harrington Crusade. Soon afterwards he rejoined me as a permanent member of my show, a better entertainer, a much wiser man, and a very happy man. He is now a featured performer in our concerts, and an exciting show-stopper.

But it wasn't Gordon Terry nor myself who turned out to be the star of the show that first time we played San Quentin. It was my guitarist, Luther Perkins. To quote Merle Haggard, "You had laryngitis, John. You told us (the inmates) that you had played a club in Brisbane the evening before, then roared till morning. You didn't sound bad, but you didn't sound right. The cons understood you'd had a big night the night before and were about wasted. Nobody said anything bad about you, though, because everyone appreciated your coming too much to criticize the shape you were in.

"There were about forty guys in the joint (San Quentin) who played a guitar, and the day after the show every one of them were trying to pick like Luther."

Merle Haggard was paroled after three years, was given a break by country singer Wynne Stewart, and went on to become one of the all-time greats in country music. He is one "star" in our business who has always tried to give credit where credit was due — to his supporting musicians and the imperative contributions they make to his stardom.

"I feel the same way about Roy Nichols as you did about Luther Perkins," Merle said one day. "I hate to think of ever trying to do a show without Roy playing guitar for me."

Merle's attitude of appreciation for his supporting men is so important. Ernest Tubb had Billy Byrd, Roy Acuff has Oswald, Hank Williams had Don Helms, and Bill Monroe once had a banjo player named Earl Scruggs. When sidemen receive the recognition they deserve, it can only make the leader a bigger man.

"We can learn a lot from the old-timers," Merle said.

"It all comes down to charity," I thought to myself. "It's the same old lesson: you gain by giving."

The concert recorded at Folsom Prison in February, 1968, was our second appearance at Folsom. Back in 1966, Rev. Gressett had asked me on behalf of the inmates he had met and counseled there to come and give a performance. Because of the response, I had talked for two years about possibly recording an album in a prison. After the first concert, I was invited to come back any time and do the recorded concert.

Now that I had stopped taking pills, I was better able to put such ideas in motion and follow through with them. Robert Johnston was my record producer at the time, and he became excited over the idea when I mentioned it to him. He made the arrangements with the record company and the prison authorities, and on February 10, 1968, we were off to Sacramento.

In the motel a few miles from Folsom Prison, we had a rehearsal. There were the Statler Brothers, Carl Perkins, the Tennessee Three (Marshall Grant, Luther Perkins, and W. S. Holland — Luther and Carl Perkins are no relation), and June Carter.

We went through a rundown of the show I planned to do the next morning, finishing the rehearsal about midnight. I stopped by the coffee shop afterwards and sat for a few minutes talking with June.

"Do you think we're moving in the right direction, John?" she asked.

"I think so," I said. "This is something I've wanted to do for years, and I feel right about it."

"I've been praying that everything will work out tomorrow," she said. "I don't think it's ever been done before. You can't tell what it will sound like, recording in a prison dining room."

"I've been praying too, June," I said. "Not only about the album tomorrow, but about a lot of things. I've been thinking a lot about you and me, about how much you mean to me."

She smiled at me. "You'd better get some sleep. We have to be at the prison at 8:00 A.M."

Just as I was going to bed, Rev. Gressett knocked on my door. When I opened it, he stuck a tape recording in my hand.

"I know you've got a lot on your mind," he said, "but I'd be doing you an injustice if I didn't ask you to listen to this song tonight."

"Tonight?" I asked sleepily.

"Tonight," he said. "Good night."

The name on the tape box was Glen Sherley. He was an inmate at Folsom. The name of the song was *Greystone Chapel,* a song about the prison church. I played it over and over and over for an hour before I went to sleep.

The M. C. for the concert was Hugh Cherry, radio man, writer, and an old friend to everybody in my business. He had flown up from Los Angeles. Hugh "warmed up" the audience, introduced my group, Rev. Gressett, and my father, who had come up to witness the live recording.

Hugh told the prison audience, "When Johnny Cash comes out, don't applaud, please. Let him introduce himself, then react naturally."

I stepped to the microphone and said, "Hello, I'm Johnny Cash," and Luther Perkins kicked off the song *Folsom Prison Blues.* Thus began the making of what I might vainly call recording history. The album sold between five and six million copies, and the single record sold another two million.

Glen Sherley had been pointed out to me. He was sitting on the front row, applauding and laughing it up with those around him.

"Men," I said, "last night about bedtime Rev. Gressett brought me a song written by one of you." I glanced at Glen Sherley. He had no idea yet.

"This is one of the most important songs to me that I've ever heard," I continued. "This song has *hope* in it. Hope that many of you need. I want to thank Glen Sherley for sending me this great song. Glen, if you don't mind, we want to try your song now."

His face turned red at first and his mouth fell open, then he turned pale. By the end of the song he was crying. He was finally making some kind of a contribution after thirteen years in prison.

> There's a Greystone Chapel here at Folsom,
> A house of worship in this den of sin,
> You wouldn't think God had a place here at Folsom,
> But He's saved the soul of many lost men.

> Inside the walls of prison my body may be,
> But the Lord has set my soul free.
> By Glen Sherley, © 1968 Southwind Music, Inc. Used by permission.
> All rights administered by Hill and Range Songs, Inc.

The show went off without a hitch. The prisoners were returned to their cells, and we boarded the bus to leave for the motel.

I turned to June. "I have a feeling that lots of good things are beginning to happen to us."

"It's time, John," she said. "We had our forty years in the wilderness. We were allowed to go through the fire for some reason. I have a feeling the album recorded today will be a big one."

"What is that verse that goes, 'Seek ye first the kingdom . . .'?" I began.

". . . of God and His righteousness and all these things shall be added unto you," she finished.

My daddy had leaned back in his seat, enjoying himself, as he does anywhere he goes. I had asked him to come along on this trip, and he had been eager to come. I was awfully proud that he could see me do a totally sober concert. It had been a long time since he'd seen me perform.

He was quiet, feeling a little bit of what we all were feeling: How great to be able to drive right through those prison gates into the free world.

"That was quite a day, wasn't it, daddy?" I asked.

"You did mighty good, son," he answered.

"Thank you, sir."

14 / **Letter to a Friend**

With a respectable life style established, and
working on the new home in Hendersonville, I was
permitted to bring my girls back from California for a short
visit. It was one of the happiest times of my life.

Sensing my new-found peace and well-being, the
girls immediately made themselves at home. They
laughed and played and treated me like I'd never been
gone. My oldest, Rosanne, was thirteen, Kathleen,
twelve, Cindy, nine, and Tara was six.

The weather was bitter cold. I built a big fire in the
fireplace and popped popcorn, and we all sat around on
the floor hoping it would snow.

June was living a few miles away in Madison with
her daughters, Carlene, twelve, and Rosey, nine. About
the time the snow started, June and her girls came out. Our
daughters were introduced and made friends right
away, as June set about getting the beds ready in the big,
round front bedroom where my girls would sleep.

Then, we missed Tara. I searched the house over
and finally found her outside, standing under a light
watching the snow fall. She had her face turned up to the
sky, letting the snowflakes fall on her face.

"It's awfully cold out here, isn't it, Tara?" I asked, reluctant to spoil the scene.

"It's so beautiful, daddy," she said. "I've never seen snow before. I thought I'd seen everything God makes, like rain and trees and grass, but I never saw snow before, and it's the most beautiful of all."

I stood there with her for awhile, savoring this rare moment; quiet times of peace and closeness had been few and far between in my life for the last seven years.

"The snow is getting deeper," June said when Tara and I came back inside. "If you don't mind, my girls and I will just spend the night. I'll sleep on the floor with all six of them."

When bedtime finally came and I went up to my room alone, I was awake for a long time. I stood quietly at the window, looking out at the white flakes falling across the lake. The cold wind was whipping the snow into deep drifts around the house.

Tomorrow would be a good day to go rabbit hunting. It would be easy to track them in the snow as I had often done as a boy. But the idea of killing something was repulsive to me. "This is no longer the time for dying," I thought. "This is the time for living and growing."

I undressed and got on my knees beside the bed, but the words wouldn't come. I couldn't put into human language all the things for which I wanted to thank Him: for the peace I was feeling now; for the years He had pulled me through; for the bright future; for life itself. I stayed that way for a long, long time, kneeling with my head in my hands, my mind racing back over the years touching on every wrong I could remember doing, clearing my conscience of it.

The present came into focus. The words still wouldn't come. But my mind was thanking Him for a million blessings that I couldn't see I deserved for any reason.

My mind also probed the future, and I put it in His hands — told Him by wordless thoughts that I'd do whatever He showed me I should do.

"Only don't give up on me," I prayed silently. "I can't make it without You."

I lay on my back in perfect peace and watched the snowflakes covering the skylight over the bed. I felt a new power.

I had humbled myself before in this room, but this time it was different. The other time I had made this room a self-imposed prison to hold me while I fought the drug demons. I had climbed these walls, literally, looking for pills in the high cornices. I had turned this bed over and, like a whimpering pup, had finally given up and called on God to handle it.

Tonight I feasted on the fruits of victory. I lay at peace on the bed. I had spent thirty minutes in silent communion with the Rock of Ages, and I felt His strength as I went to sleep.

"June, will you marry me?"

It wasn't at a remote table in the corner by candlelight. It was onstage in London, Ontario, the next week, before five thousand people! For some reason, I had more nerve to officially ask her onstage than I would have had privately.

She glared at me in pleasant disbelief.

I repeated the question. "Will you marry me? I love you."

Then she was embarrassed. "Let's go on with the show," she said.

But the audience was in on the act by now, and they started calling out, "Say yes! Say yes!"

"You have to answer me," I said.

A slow smile came on her face. "All right," she said. "Yes, I will."

I kissed her lightly and whispered, "I couldn't help it. It was time to ask."

"Let's sing another song," she whispered back.

"Here is a song I believe is very appropriate right now," I said.

John: If I were a carpenter, and you were a lady,
Would you marry me anyway, would you have my baby?

June: If you were a carpenter, and I were a lady,
I'd marry you anyway, I'd have your baby.

John: If I were a miller, and a mill wheel grinding,
Would you miss your colored blouse,
And your soft shoes shining?

June: If you were a miller, and a mill wheel grinding,
I'd not miss my colored blouse,
And my soft shoes shining.

John: If a tinker was my trade,
Would I still find you?

June: I'd be carrying the pots you made,
Following behind you.

By Tim Hardin, © Hudson Bay Music. Used by permission.

London, Ontario, is the hometown of Saul Holiff, who was my manager at the time and had been for several years. From time to time Saul had tried to advise June and me on personal things as well as on business affairs. We had long ago found an understanding friend in Saul. He had suffered much embarrassment because of some of my capers when I was on pills. But he was cool, level-headed, and always handled the most complicated

of my business problems without burdening me down
with the details of what he'd gone through in straightening
out some of the messes I got myself into from missing
show dates. He had never relayed the embarrassing
questions he must have had to answer when I'd
been in trouble.

I'd never seen him as happy as he was that night in
London after the show. "How long has it been now?" he
asked me when I came offstage.

"Over three months since I had a pill, Saul," I
said.

"Well, I heard that little proposal out there
tonight, and let me be the first to congratulate you.
You've lost a lot in the last seven years. You need June, and
she needs you now. You've proven everybody wrong,
including me. I thought you would have been dead by
now."

"I would have been, Saul, if God hadn't saved
me," I said.

"And that brings up a subject I need to talk to you
about," Saul said. "Reconciliation with God does not
necessarily mean you are reconciled with man."

"I'm working on that, too," I said. "There's no
way I can make amends to every person I've offended or
hurt, but wherever I can, I will. I'll just do the best I can,
and maybe eventually the good will outweigh the bad.
And that statement is not a cop-out. I know there are some
wrongs I've done that cannot be reconciled by trying to
be and do better now."

"You might consider playing some shows for a
couple of promoters who went broke when you canceled
out on them," Saul said.

"Arrange them," I said. "Any legitimate debt I
owe, I'll pay. It's more important to *me* to clean the slate
than it is for you or anyone else."

"OK, but I doubt that," Saul said, and he stood
looking at June and me a moment. "Who are they going

to gossip about in Nashville now?" he asked with a smile.

"I don't know," I said, returning the smile, "but it's time they found someone else, and there are quite a few likely prospects in town."

June and I were married March 1, 1968, at a church in Franklin, Kentucky, just north of Nashville. Hundreds of relatives, friends, and music people came to the reception at the lakeside house that evening. Merle Kilgore was best man at our wedding.

At the wedding reception he was the life of the party. We didn't serve alcohol, but he was high on life and happiness at seeing an old friend back among the living.

"Let's take off these neckties, Kilgore," I said.

"Naw, leave it on for June," he said.

"No, I'll leave it on for you," I said. "June loves me without a tie."

He was about the last one to leave that night. As he walked out to his car, he yelled back, "You sure you don't remember his name, Cash?"

"Whose name?" I asked.

"The Pharaoh of Egypt!" he laughed.

In 1968 many changes came about — some good, some bad — but through it all, June and I lived the happiest year of our lives.

We stuck together like glue. I gathered strength and gained a little spiritual growth from Bible study and long discussions with June about the Bible, and mainly about Jesus and His teachings.

We got interested in Jewish history, especially as it related to the Bible. We studied Josephus, the Jewish historian. We read *The Robe, Ben Hur, Quo Vadis, Spartacus,* and all the books by Taylor Caldwell and Thomas B. Costain that had as their setting the time of Christ. I crammed a hunger that had been gnawing for years with new biblical knowledge.

In the month of June we toured Europe again, this time in concert halls in Frankfort, Munich, Hamburg, Glasgow, Dublin, Manchester, and the Palladium in London.

After the tour, June and I went to Israel for a week as tourists. We took a tape recorder and visited many places sacred to Christians, Jews, and Moslems, recording our thoughts and impressions along the way. We cherished the very earth we walked upon, remembering the great events of the life of Christ. And when we read the Bible, it came vividly alive from our having walked and explored the places where He walked.

It was soon after returning from the long European tour and our week in Israel that Luther Perkins died following burns in a fire in his home. The loss that Marshall, W. T., and I felt was staggering.

"How can we even think about going on without him?" Marshall said that day after the funeral.

"I'll do all I can to help," said Carl Perkins, "but nobody can ever take Luther's place."

Every guitar player in our business mourned Luther's passing.

Concerts were booked, but I wouldn't even talk about replacing Luther. Carl Perkins did fill in as lead guitarist, as he had offered to — until two months later backstage at Fayetteville, Arkansas. That night, June, W. S. Holland, and I had driven in. Marshall and Carl Perkins were to fly in from Memphis, but their plane was grounded due to bad weather.

Show time came and there was only June, W. S., and me. "We'll have to do the best we can, W. S.," I said. "You're the band tonight."

He looked out at the seven thousand people waiting. "My big opportunity to be a star," he said, laughing.

Then a young, black-haired man named Bob

Wootton introduced himself. He reminded me of my self-assured approach to Sam Phillips at Sun records thirteen years earlier when he said, "You need me. I can play all your songs."

"Do you play like Luther?" I asked.

"Nobody can do that," he said. "But I'll try if you want me to."

"Get out there and plug your guitar in," I said.

Onstage Bob played every song I called out to him, exactly as it had been recorded and even in the key in which it had been recorded.

"Key of C!" I yelled at him toward the end of the show as he kicked off a song in what I thought was the wrong key.

"You recorded it in D!" he yelled back.

I stopped the song. "But I want to sing it in C," I said.

"OK," he said reluctantly, beginning again in the key of C. "But you recorded it in D."

After the show he asked for the job. I told him to give me a couple of days to think it over and I'd call him.

Marshall had been with me since the beginning, as Luther had. The Tennessee Two, they had called themselves. W. S. Holland had worked with Carl Perkins at the beginning, but W. S. had decided not to work on the road any more following an auto accident in 1957. A few months afterwards, however, I asked him to join our group, and the Tennessee Two became the Tennessee Three.

The next day after Fayetteville, I said to W. S., "That guitar player Wootton was all right, don't you think?"

"I can't get over it," W. S. said. "Sometimes it's like you're living your life by a script that's long been written. Marshall and Carl couldn't get there, so you had no guitar player. It's the first show Carl has ever missed.

Suddenly there appears a guitar player who has trained himself to do a perfect job for you, and he appears on the night no one is there to play guitar. Any other time you wouldn't have listened to him, much less put him onstage with you."

"I like him," said June. "He sounds a little like Luther, but he's got a sound all his own."

"And a mind all his own," I said. "Did you hear him argue with me about what key I was going to sing in?"

"Let's call him to join us tonight so Marshall and Carl can hear him," June suggested.

I wouldn't have considered hiring someone new without the approval of Marshall, Carl, W. S., and June. One big reason for the failure and break-up of so many bands and groups is the inability of musicians and performers to get along together. It isn't only important to be able to perform together; it's important to be able to *live* together, day after day in cars, buses, planes, hotels; to go that extra mile for each other, to adapt, to compromise personal needs and tastes, to share, to treat everyone in the group as if they are blood brother or sister. Because to stay together and get along as we had for all these years, we were closer than brothers and sisters.

Marshall and Carl approved of Bob Wootton from the minute they met him.

"I wouldn't have thought we'd ever find another guitar player who could fill the bill," said Marshall. "Let's take him along if you want to. We'll find out in time if we can live together."

(Marshall told me later, "We boarded two different flights in Memphis that would have connected to Fayetteville, and they were both canceled because of weather. The third plane we boarded, which would have gotten us there, was grounded because of mechanical trouble just as we were about to take off.

"Carl and I got off and chartered a small jet, but by the time we were airborne the show was underway without us. Everything worked out in Wootton's favor to provide him with the opportunity to work with us.")

One thing I came to appreciate about Bob was his knowledge of and love for the hymns and gospel songs I'd recorded. He knew them all, as well as everything else I'd ever done. This, and his easy-going manner and ability to adjust and get along with people, plus his love for and devotion to his job, cinched his position with us.

He, also, is now like a brother to me — as a matter of fact, he *is* a brother-in-law, having married Anita Carter in 1974.

Tour followed tour, the crowds increased, moral debts were paid, and previously missed engagements were made good. I reestablished contact with and made amends to some that I could remember offending. People were thanked. People like Rev. Gressett and Sheriff Ralph Jones and Nat Winston and E. J. and Maybelle Carter and my parents.

I began to realize, as I had expected, that some people could forgive and forget, but others couldn't. Aboard a plane from Nashville to Washington, I sat down by singer Jimmy Dean. We carried on a little small talk most of the way, talking about this and that in the music business.

Jimmy was going on to New York, and it wasn't until we were landing in Washington that he said, "I never saw your eyes so clear before. I don't think you ever looked me straight in the eye like you've been doing today."

I felt this was the opening line of a conversation he had been wanting to bring up. "I've no reason not to look you in the eye," I said.

"I'm not so sure about that," said Jimmy. "I've

been mad at you for years, and I think it's time I told you
so. I hear a lot about your religion, but I don't think your
straight living now can make up for all the damage
you've done to lots of people in the music business,
including myself. I've been refused rooms in hotels
because 'Johnny Cash had been there and tore the place
up.' You hurt my business, Cash.''

He was talking low and slow and deliberate, as if
he was finally getting something off his chest that he had
waited a long time to say.

I weighed my answer. A million things raced
through my mind that I could say; things that I *would*
have said in reply to such a statement from a fellow
entertainer a few years earlier. But I knew Jimmy Dean
was speaking not only for himself, but for many others in
my business who hadn't had the courage or concern to
tell me. Now it was time for me to show my concern and
courage.

"You're right, Jimmy," I said. "I'm sorry."

The plane was at the gate. Everyone was off that
was getting off, except myself, and Jimmy and I were
standing in the aisle now.

Jimmy was smiling — no, grinning. There was a
little bond of show-business brotherhood and artist
appreciation on both our parts that couldn't be denied.
"It's good to see you looking so healthy," he said.

I shook his hand and said, "I hope you won't stay
mad long."

"Naw," he said, shrugging it off. "But I would
like to sit down with you sometime and have a long talk
about all these things I hear have happened to you. I'm not
sure I understand nor believe a lot of it."

"I'm not sure you should believe a lot of it," I
said. "But a lot of good things have happened. Call me
when you come to Nashville. Let's get together."

He sat back down and said, "Keep your eyes
clear, Cash."

I knew that I must have caused my own brothers
and sisters, especially Tommy, a lot of embarrassment.
Being an entertainer, he must have faced a barrage of
questions from his fans and mine.

Tommy has long been headlining his own
show and has a good reputation for neatness and
dependability. We managed to work a few shows together,
and during one of our long conversations one night at
dinner I tried to apologize to him for shaming the
family name.

He said, "You don't owe me an apology for
anything you've done wrong. I was only concerned with
what you were doing to yourself — the whole family was.
But let me tell you," he continued, "at times it's been
fun being your brother. At other times it's been well —
interesting."

"You've handled it well, Tom," I said. "You're a
good man."

"You're not so bad yourself, John — now," he
said.

"I hope you'll always be proud of me, as I am of
you," I said.

"Pass the bread and change the subject," he said.

On New Year's Eve 1968 I sat down and wrote
myself a letter, as I have done on every New Year's Eve
since then.

That New Year's Eve I said, in part:

> Hendersonville, Tennessee
> January 1, 1969
>
> Dear Cash,
> . . . let's look at 1968. You did all right in
> a lot of ways. You blew it in others. . . .
> You stayed off pills but you're still awfully
> carnal. You know what those little vices
> of yours are. Get to work on them before they

multiply and lower your resistance to other
temptations—like pills, for instance. . . . You
can't lie to me, you know. You still think
about them from time to time. You need to
pray more. You hardly ever pray. . . .
Big deals ahead in 1969, possibly a network
TV show, but the biggest deal you've got
going is your family and home. You'd better
hang with God if you want the other
deals to work out. . . .

Your friend,
Cash

15 / **The Hounds of Hell**

Our boys were in Vietnam. Our friend, country singer Jan Howard, had lost a son, Jimmy, in the war. Jimmy was loved by all who knew him — a popular boy in school, a quiet boy at home, a "good boy." June and I had been with Jan during the terribly trying time of the funeral and afterwards.

When a request came from promoters to tour the Far East, Vietnam bases included, June and I decided to go. "There are thousands of boys over there just like Jimmy Howard," June said. "They're there because their country sent them."

"They're talking about us playing ballrooms, clubs, June," I said. "We haven't played clubs in years. Okinawa, Philippines, Vietnam, Japan — officers' and enlisted men's clubs at the American bases."

"Do you want to do it?" she asked.

"They say security will be no problem in Vietnam," I said. "But we won't go unless you want to."

"I can stand it if you can," she said.

"I think we should," I decided.

We stopped over in Hawaii for two days, then on to Okinawa for three. It was cold, wet, and rainy in Okinawa, and what with two shows a night in the smoke-filled clubs and doing extra-long shows for the highly enthusiastic servicemen, I found myself exhausted and down with a bad cold by the time we left Okinawa.

We had visited military hospitals in Okinawa, and June had taken dozens of wounded servicemen's names and home phone numbers with the promise, "I'll call your mother," or "I'll call your wife and say you're okay." When we got back to the States, she spent two days doing just that.

When we arrived in Manila, I had a slight fever with lung congestion. But I had the night off so I took aspirin and went right to bed while June went out shopping.

"Two shows tomorrow night at the naval base in Subic Bay. How will I ever be able to sing?" I thought. "I'd better call the hotel doctor and get a shot of antibiotics."

The doctor came up, took my temperature, examined me, and gave me a shot with instructions to stay in bed. And just as he was walking out the door, I said, "Doctor, I have to do two shows tomorrow night. Can you give me something I can take to help me get through them?"

"Like what?" he asked.

"Dexedrine or Dexamyl," I said. "Something mild that won't hurt me."

"Let me see what I have," he said, looking in his bag.

He handed me a couple dozen samples of Dexamyl capsules, the twelve-hour jobs. "This is all I have," he said. "Don't take more than one a day." And he was gone.

"Take one," said Deception. "It will help dry up the congestion."

I had forgotten what it had been like on pills. I only knew I was miserably sick now, and I told myself, "I'll follow the doctor's instructions and take only one. I'll feel better, and no one will know. It won't hurt a thing.''

I had been sick, feverish, and with the whirlwind tour of concerts I was doing in the clubs, my resistance was weakened further by the very influence of my environment.

When June returned, I was up and dressed. Five capsules were in my pocket. The rest, a dozen and a half, were hidden in my suitcase.

"Oh, you're feeling better. I'm so glad," she said, not yet suspecting pills.

We went out to dinner, and I picked at my food, having lost my appetite. I felt feverish again after I ate a few bites, so I excused myself and went to the rest room.

I looked at myself in the mirror. My eyes were only slightly dilated. June would think it was from the cold and fever. I started to walk out to rejoin her, but turned quickly around and swallowed another twelve-hour capsule of Dexedrine.

When we got back to the hotel, June was worried. "Please lay down and go to sleep," she begged. "You'll be unable to work tomorrow night."

I finally did lay down, but only to keep her from knowing what I'd done. I didn't sleep all night and kept her awake most of the night tossing and turning.

Next morning early, as we left for the long drive to the officers' club at Subic Bay, I knew I looked terrible. I had thought about the Dexedrine all night.

Deception said, "Take two more as soon as you get up and you'll feel great."

The devil was way ahead in this round of my life's battle, so I took two when I got up, and by the time the long nightmare of a trip to Subic Bay was over, June knew what was the matter. She didn't say yet, but I knew she knew. She sat in a corner, head down.

I'd called a waiter to come to the back room of the

officers' club where we were waiting to go onstage that night. "Bring me a double shot of brandy," I said. "I've got to clear my throat."

June turned pale.

She walked over and whispered to me, "Oh, no, John. Not brandy mixed with whatever you've already taken. You know what it'll do to you."

"Mind your own business," I said, gulping the brandy down. "I've got a show to do."

The lights blinded me when I walked onstage. I found the microphone and whispered, "Hello, I'm Johnny Cash." Applause, handclapping, foot stomping, whistling.

But when the spotlight came on me, I said, "I can't sing much. I've got a bad cold and fever, but I'll do my best."

"Sing," they cheered. *"Folsom Prison Blues, I Walk the Line."*

I struggled through an hour show, trying to sing everything they requested.

At the enlisted men's club, two hours later, the whole scene was repeated. I took another capsule, another double shot of brandy. The only difference was I didn't remember much of the show. When June came on singing *Jackson* with me, she tried to smile and couldn't.

I remember well the scene afterwards when I lay down on the seat of the bus with my head in her lap on the way back to the hotel in Manila. She cried most of the way, wiping my face with cold towels and gently stroking my scalp with her fingers.

"See what happened, John," she said. "Please throw them away."

"I took them all," I said, not counting the dozen and a half hidden in my suitcase back at the hotel.

I was in such misery from the mixture of alcohol and an overdose of amphetamines that I couldn't lie still.

My skin was crawling, muscle spasms twisted and tortured my back and neck. Finally June called the hotel doctor, a different one, and he gave me a shot to counteract the Dexedrine to put me to sleep.

I was still groggy at plane time the next day and weak from loss of rest and lack of food. But I made it aboard the plane and slept until we reached Saigon. We had the night off, and the military police took us to the officers' club for dinner, then to house trailers which they had provided for our quarters while we were at Long Binh Air Force Base.

It was summertime in January in Vietnam. The temperature was over 100°, and before bedtime my temperature was up as well. When they took me to the base hospital, X-rays showed I had pneumonia. I got more antibiotics, then returned to my trailer.

I remembered the dozen and a half capsules were in an envelope in my suitcase. I stuffed them down in the couch, intending to leave them there. And I did leave them there for four days and nights, because with dark that evening came another sobering experience.

June and I went to bed early and were almost asleep when we heard the first shell explode. The mortar blasts, the rifles, and the shelling went on all night long. The rounds came in so close to Long Binh they shook our trailer. We slept very little with the terrible din going on so nearby. At daylight the shelling stopped.

We went back to the hospital next morning and started making the rounds visiting the sick and wounded. We watched as they brought them in from the hospital helicopter pads — terrible scenes of suffering. We tried to visit every bed in the hospital. Carl Perkins brought along his guitar, and he, June, and I stopped in several wards and sang a few songs.

By show time my fever was higher, and three shows were scheduled. I thought of the amphetamines, but fought against the urge to take them.

The looks on the faces of those young soldiers that I played to gave me courage. They crowded around the stage that evening, whistled, stomped their feet, some of them even cried with joy that someone had come from "home" to entertain them. They let off more steam than a prison audience. Each audience was more enthusiastic than the last, more grateful for our coming.

On the morning we were to leave for Tokyo, I was up early, feeling much better after all the sweating I'd done in eighteen or twenty concerts. I sat down on the couch and reached into the upholstery and found the capsules. I put them in my pocket. Drinking my coffee, I sat there thinking about what I had gone through in the last week and feeling a little proud of myself for having done all those shows. Now there was only one more to do. A concert tonight at Tachikawa Air Force Base near Tokyo. "That one will be a breeze," I thought, "after what we've been through." The only thing I dreaded was the long flight to Tokyo. I knew it would be exhausting.

"You deserve to enjoy the trip. Have a couple of capsules of Dexedrine," said a demon called Pride. "It's *your* business and nobody else's," said Arrogance.

"Right. Nobody will know," said my old tormentor Deception.

I took two twenty-milligram capsules. By the time we reached the Saigon airport, June knew I'd done it again because the medication hit me harder than I'd anticipated.

I talked a mile a minute to our driver all the way there and immediately got laryngitis again. When I got out of the car at the terminal, I was staggering and fumbling and mumbling. June was quiet — a hurt, resigned quiet. The day was a heavy load on her shoulders.

At the terminal I came face to face with Rev. Jimmy Snow, pastor of Evangel Temple in Nashville and a friend from the fifties. I had known him before he started preaching. He had had a pill problem before he became a Christian, and I knew there was no fooling him. "He'll know I'm on pills," I thought before I said a word.

"What a place to run into you," I said. "What are you doing in Vietnam?"

"Preaching and singing," Jimmy said. "Are you doing concerts here?"

"We just finished," June said quickly. "John has pneumonia."

"Yeah, I'm really sick," I whispered.

"Well, I've got to catch my plane," Jimmy said, shaking my hand and looking me straight in the eye. He disappeared toward his plane.

When I got on board our flight, I headed for the rest room. I looked at myself in the mirror. "Jimmy Snow knew. June knows. Who do you think you're fooling?"

"Who cares?" said Arrogance.

Two more capsules and I knew I wouldn't care.

We arrived two hours late at the club at Tachikawa Air Force Base. June sat in the back seat crying all the way to the base, but I wasn't concerned with her feelings.

I could only whisper when I stumbled into the stage door of the club — a big club, possibly two thousand drinking, yelling, handclapping servicemen wanting a show.

I thought I had lost my mind, and I almost sobered when I walked backstage and heard myself singing *Greystone Chapel.* At least it sounded exactly like me.

Actually the singer was a Japanese friend of mine named Takahiro Saito whom I had met on my first trip to Japan in 1961. He knew all my songs, and he was doing all of them, trying to please the audience that kept yelling my name.

"Maybe I won't have to go on," I thought. But Saito had seen me and was introducing me.

I staggered out to the microphone, shook Saito's hand, and in an almost inaudible rasp, said, "Hello, I'm Johnny Cash."

Then followed the saddest, most humbling hour of my life.

The noisy, roaring, clapping, whistling, yelling, drinking mob of two thousand servicemen listened silently in disbelief as I whispered *Folsom Prison Blues, I Walk the Line, Ring of Fire,* and the rest.

I stood in one spot to keep from falling on my face and whispered my songs. After an hour of that hell I closed the show with, "I'm sorry I was late, men, and I'm sorry I was in such bad shape. You'll never see me this way again," and I walked off.

Back in the hotel, I said to June, "I don't know how long before I'll be able to sleep. I took six, maybe eight of them today and tonight."

"Let's pray," June said.

We knelt by the bed, and I repented. We prayed for strength and healing, and the Great Physician worked a healing miracle because in the bed we held each other tight, and I was sound asleep in June's arms before I knew it.

The next day when we awoke, I showed her the capsules I had left. "I'm going to flush these myself," I said, and I did — all of them.

The lesson I learned on the Far East tour was learned well. The lesson: God is love and God is forgiving. He'll forgive you seventy times seven and seventy times that. He is long-suffering, patient, compassionate, and He understands even before you try to explain your weaknesses and shortcomings to Him. When you stand with Him, you must renew the stand daily; you must daily be on guard. The hounds of hell are not going to stop snapping at your heels. The devil and his demons aren't going to give up on you as long as they can find a vulnerable spot once in awhile.

It's been a daily battle to overcome, but the fight gets more interesting all the time. I've learned not to laugh at the devil, but I must say that since that day in January of 1969, I have never touched amphetamines again. No kind of them — no color, no five, ten, or twenty-milligram ones, no heart-shaped ones, no round ones, no yellow ones, no green ones, no black ones — none at all.

16 / **A Better Bubble**

That temporary setback in the Far East was something June and I never discussed — not with the others on the show, not even between ourselves. To even bring it up, we knew, would be giving undue recognition to those dark and negative forces. I wouldn't acknowledge to anyone but June, myself, and God that I had lost a round right in the middle of a long winning streak.

Yet I surely did admit it to myself. For to deny that I had stumbled would itself be another error.

But we profited from the mistake. Through His wisdom and understanding, I felt a greater victory than ever over drugs — even immediately following the bad time. I saw clearly how I'd been tempted, how I'd fallen, and the relapse into the old way was short enough that I could closely examine the details of it all in my own mind.

In searching His understanding, I marveled that He hadn't let me die. But the more I searched, the more I knew He had been with me in Manila, in Vietnam, and even in Tokyo when I had been the most negative and evil man I could ever remember being. My man-pride and arrogance had vanished the minute I humbled myself enough to call on Him, and I didn't have to wait long. The calming, cleansing peace and forgiveness swept me like a baptism, and I had slept like a baby that night in Tokyo.

June and I lived in (if you'll pardon the corny expression) wedded bliss. Carlene and Rosey loved the lakeside home. My girls were able to come from time to time, and other times I visited them in California.

Columbia Records asked me to record another album in a prison, and a concert was arranged at San Quentin.

Don Davis, a Nashville music publisher, called me the day before I was leaving for San Quentin. "I know you get a lot of songs pitched to you," he said, "and I wouldn't bother you if I didn't know you'd want this song."

"What is it?" I asked.

"It's called *A Boy Named Sue*," he said. "It was written by Shel Silverstein."

"Bring it on out," I said, thinking Don Davis must be wrong this time. It sounded like something I *knew* I wouldn't want.

When he played it, though, I knew he was right. But the morning we left, I had so much on my mind that I wouldn't have even taken the lyrics to *A Boy Named Sue* if June hadn't reminded me.

I didn't have time to learn it, so at San Quentin I laid the lyrics on the floor in front of me and read them off, one time through with no rehearsal.

"I have a new song," I said. "I don't know it yet, but I'll sing it to you as best I can."

A Boy Named Sue and the San Quentin album surpassed the Folsom Prison record success, making Johnny Cash Columbia Records' biggest selling artist in 1969, with over six million albums sold, and half that many single records.

The profanity on that record was written into the lyrics, and I went ahead and sang the "s.o.b." — which later was bleeped out. It was taking a little while, a little growth, for a cleaner language to catch up with my new nature. I should have remembered that when I made a mistake, the whole world will know about it.

Music business and entertainment world successes and achievements came so fast that it was hard to keep up with the direction in which I was going.

When the offer came from ABC for a network television show we felt right about it as an opportunity to do the music we loved doing and to do it for millions of people.

I enjoyed the television shows for the most part. I was able to work with some great talent who were guests on the show, and I was able to have many of my friends on the show, and many more who became friends.

Two guests I was most proud to have with me on the show were Merle Haggard and Charlie Pride. Both had made it big and were two of the most sought-after performers in our business.

Merle Haggard never changed. Always grateful for the adulation of his fans, he consistently maintained his humble, easygoing manner. He stands tall as an inspiration to all underdogs, especially prisoners. He is a symbol of human hope for countless thousands.

And even though I was a couple of years late, I felt I was making up in part at least for that big lie I'd told Charlie Pride about getting him on the Grand Ole Opry. (This wasn't the Grand Ole Opry — he had long since made that on his own without my help — this was my show. But it was done at the Grand Ole Opry *House!*)

The first show we taped was the greatest joy of my career. I walked out on the stage prior to the taping of the show and received a standing ovation — the stage I had been banned from four years before.

The Grand Ole Opry manager was there to shake my hand when I came off. Not a word was said, but we were both very happy.

Being in America's living room every week via TV, singing songs I felt were right for me, songs I believed my audience wanted to hear, I was talking to the heart of my audience through hymns and the "Ride This Train" segment. I became, in many ways, public property, and our home became a public attraction.

Mike Nesmith, who at the time was with the Monkees and a guest on the show, told me over breakfast at our home, "So now you're a superstar, John. Want to make a bet on how long your marriage will last, how long you'll have this beautiful home?"

That challenge of Mike's has been one of the most important things ever said to me.

"Why shouldn't it last?" I asked.

"Fame is fleeting," he said, "and when it flies, it takes its trappings with it."

"My marriage and this home are not fame's trappings, Mike," I said. "God gave us all this, and if He wants to take it away, fine. But as for our marriage and our home, He is the seal, He is the bond. If we hang with Him like we plan to, it will hold."

"Well, you may have something there," Mike said. "I've seen a lot of worldly bubbles burst. Maybe yours won't, if it isn't all worldly."

"It isn't all worldly, Mike," I said. "I won't bet with you, but watch us and see for yourself, OK?"

"OK, I'll be pulling for you," Mike said. "Hope you've got a better bubble."

Thousands of cards and letters came in every week. We bought a large building a mile from home, and my sister Reba moved back from California and began handling public relations and in general coordinated my personal appointments.

She hired a staff of people to take care of the mail and public contacts. She organized House of Cash music publishing company, and with Larry Lee, an old friend, got the company underway successfully. We built a recording studio in the building, a big beautiful one which June decorated in blue.

Reba became my right arm in many business and personal affairs. I sought her advice and followed her recommendation on many problems that arose. I felt safe with Reba, a level-headed, practicing Christian, handling things.

Artist Consultants of California handled my personal appearances; the agency APA handled television and films; and Reba assisted me personally in clearing dates and helping me arrange my schedule.

A flood of requests came for appearances for charity, for churches, for preachers, for prisons, for drug centers — personal pleas for needy people in all walks of life. It seemed at times that the burdens of the world lay on my desk — a spot where I rarely had time to sit. Reba, June, and I (when I could) helped go through and answer the pleas. There was never enough time to fulfill all the requests and all the legitimate needs; Johnny Cash needed to be a hundred people.

"God told me to write you," began many letters.

"God told me to come to you for help," said many people when I answered the door at any hour of the day and night.

That scared me at first. I tried to help them all, afraid not to. But finally we had to put a guard on duty around the clock to have any privacy.

"God, did you send all those people to me?" I asked, confused.

I decided that if I did my best, followed my conscience, took care of my home and family, and prayed daily for wisdom to know what to do, then I need not worry. He'd show me. I'd have to decide through communion with the Counselor how I should respond to the countless requests.

Once a man approached the guard at my gate with, "The Lord sent me to see Johnny Cash."

I was out of town, and the guard couldn't resist answering, "Didn't the Lord tell you Johnny Cash was in Pittsburgh?"

The tour buses came to my house. A few at first, then forty or fifty a day, and I enjoyed it all.

My parents moved back from California and bought a nice home in our neighborhood, but I had no idea they would be so robbed of their privacy. They missed the quiet, peaceful life in California and were a long time adjusting to the flood of people who were always at their door, wanting to take pictures or wanting to know about me. They were kind and courteous to the tourists and visitors, posing for pictures, signing autographs, and answering a million questions.

I'd always have to leave my house a few minutes early for any appointment in order to spend a few minutes meeting the people at my gate.

Only once have I lost my temper, and that was when I came home and found a strange man standing in Rosey's bedroom. Rosey had gone in before me and was standing there petrified.

"I'm not going to hurt you," he said to Rosey, grinning. He looked high on something.

"Who are you and how did you get in here?" I asked.

"I slipped in," he laughed. "The door was open. You don't know me."

I grabbed him around the head and ran, dragging him out the door, and threw him into the yard. He turned and ran.

"I don't think the Lord sent him," I growled.

In the midst of the weekly TV series, I was booked for an appearance at the Waldorf-Astoria Hotel in New York. Senators, congressmen, generals, Bob Hope, Bing Crosby, Raquel Welch, and a host of other celebrities were gathered in the palatial ballroom for a dinner honoring Mamie Eisenhower. I was a special guest on the program, and it was carried over network television.

Well, *A Boy Named Sue* had been a number one hit record. I had won all those Grammy Awards and the Country Music Awards and had a network TV show — so far as fleeting fame and earthly glories, I was on top. I'd been to Carnegie Hall, the Hollywood Bowl, and on the cover of several magazines. And I was a little bit cocky.

That afternoon at dress rehearsal everything went beautifully. The performance was just right for the television show.

Then we were called upon to attend an affair which I detest — a cocktail party. And I haven't only recently started hating cocktail parties. I have always hated them with a passion. I have never consumed a cocktail, but that isn't the reason.

Everyone seems to feel they're obligated to act as if they're enjoying themselves, standing around with that weird-looking, dainty drink in their hand with that little finger sticking out.

I can never remember anything significant ever being said at a cocktail party. Nobody really listens to anything anyone else tells them. You open a conversation with somebody, and they're looking around you to the left or right while you're talking to be sure they're not missing another celebrity.

I told one lady, "Hello, ma'am, I'm Johnny Cash my great-aunt died how are you?"

She was looking around for the President, or

somebody, and didn't even hear me. I repeated it, "I'm Johnny Cash my great-aunt died how are you?"

"Oh, hello, Mr. Cash, how darling to meet you." Then she turned to someone else that she wasn't looking at.

By the time I finished meeting and speaking to everyone, I was a nervous wreck. I was about to explode by show time.

I hit the stage that evening ready to begin my six-minute medley of songs. As I looked out over that audience, I thought I'd never seen such a sea of black formal coattails, ruffled shirts, and bow ties in my life. And over on my left about twelve feet away sat Bob Hope with Mamie Eisenhower.

I hit a lick on my guitar to kick the medley off and dropped my pick. When I reached down to retrieve the pick — I had on my Andrew Jackson outfit with long tails and tight trousers which hook under my shoes like ski pants — those trousers ripped open all the way from my knee to my crotch. It was the inside of my right leg, and Mamie Eisenhower was sitting over to the left. I glanced up at her; her face had turned red, and she was painfully keeping back a smile.

There I was, bending over trying to get that pick underneath my index fingernail, and I couldn't pick it up. I didn't have another pick so I kept on and kept on and kept on. It seemed like 180 years going by. And all the time my bare leg was showing out in front of all those people. There was muffled giggling as people tried not to laugh and not to show their pity for me in that eternity while I was bent over trying to get that pick. I went through several different phases of emotions: first came embarrassment; then fright because I couldn't get that pick up; then tension; then anger; and arrogance when I finally grabbed the pick, stood up, and got into my medley.

When I finished my songs, I couldn't smile and bow to the audience because I was so upset over the whole situation. So I ran offstage, and of course June was there and had seen what happened. She followed me into the elevator and through the halls as I stormed into our fancy big suite. I slammed the door, jerked my coat and pants off, threw them on the floor, and jumped up and down on them. I cried, cursed, yelled, refused to talk to June, and finally locked myself in the bathroom — just stood there feeling sorry for myself.

After awhile I came back out, and June was sitting in a chair way over in the corner with her head down. I sat down across the room from her and fumed.

Finally I began to calm down. She looked at me and smiled. I dropped my head refusing to smile back at her. Then I looked up again, and she smiled back at me the second time. I didn't smile back, but I held her stare this time. And then a big grin spread all over her face and she started laughing.

I got mad all over again. "What are you laughing at? What can possibly be funny?"

She kept on laughing, rocking back and forth in her chair. It was so ridiculous that I began grinning at her, then with her.

And then she calmed down and looked at me, and I knew she was about to tell me something that would make everything right.

"John," she said, "tonight the Lord busted your britches."

All of a sudden she and I were laughing, rolling on the floor in each other's arms.

I remember well the lesson that evening taught: "Beware that you brag about standing, lest you fall."

June and I were hoping to have a son, and for the first year it looked like it wasn't going to happen. Then in the middle of 1969 we went on vacation to the Virgin Islands. It was a beautiful time. Hot, sunny days on the beach and in the surf; then at night that moonlight filtered through the palm trees and worked its magic.

On the way home from the vacation, I said, "Let's name him John Carter Cash."

June laughed, "Boy, you're fast. Who says I'm pregnant?"

"I do," I said. "I just believe you are."

A few weeks later, June said out of a clear blue sky, "I just believe I am, too."

"What?" I asked.

"Pregnant," she said.

Dr. Frederec Cothren at the Madison, Tennessee, Seventh Day Adventist Hospital must have delivered thousands of babies, but before he would deliver a baby or perform an operation, this doctor knelt beside the operating table or bed, asking God to guide his hands for a safe operation or delivery. And when June entered the delivery room, he did just that.

There had been a time three years earlier when I had gone to Dr. Cothren asking for help with my pill problem. It was one of those times when I knew I was in bad shape, but not down enough to really surrender.

Though I was sincere about needing help, I had a supply of pills and wasn't quite sincere enough to throw them away. In addition to that, I couldn't resist checking him out to see if I could get more pills from him on prescription.

"Dr. Cothren," I had said, "could you give me a few samples of antidepressants, something like Dexamyl, to take in the hospital. It's going to be a battle for me."

He said, "Are you crazy? I will not give you the very thing that I know is killing you. I'll admit you to the hospital, feed you good, let you get a lot of sleep. But so far as your habit, only you can break that. Of course, you could do it easier if you'd let God help."

That three days in the hospital turned out to be a real caper. I took my pills and my guitar into the hospital with me and stayed up. At night the nurses brought me a sleeping pill, but I doubled up on the amphetamines. By the third day, Dr. Cothren warned me that if I wouldn't be quiet and get some rest he'd have to ask me to leave the hospital.

As soon as he left the room, I put on my clothes and walked out the back door. I thought I had worn out another welcome and burned another bridge, but people like Dr. Cothren have a way of forgetting and forgiving others' shortcomings. So when he came around to congratulate me on the birth of our son, I knew that the hard time he'd had with me was long forgotten.

I was working at the Grand Ole Opry when John Carter was born, taping the TV shows and rehearsing everyday. When I was free, I'd be at the hospital with June and the baby.

During that time, June and I had some long talks. We'd both been through broken marriages, and though we were very much in love, we had been through enough to know that even our marriage could be in trouble if we didn't stay together and work together.

The birth of the baby had a way of resealing the bond of our marriage, and I was reminded again by this event just how much I really needed June. I was never really whole without her, never really felt like a concert was complete without her.

I had always had the greatest respect for her as a performer, but until I'd had to do a few concerts without her during her pregnancy, I suppose I didn't realize just how much she meant to me as a fellow performer. June was always an inspiration, and I just felt like I did a better job knowing she was in the wings.

But more than that, she and I talked about the price we had paid, the fight we had fought, the ups and downs, the good times and the bad, the heartbreak and the victories, so that we might be together. I had missed so much with my daughters by being away from them. We had all suffered. But here was another chance — a new child.

June and I talked about the upcoming engagements and concerts which were booked. We both knew we had to take John Carter with us some way, that we must have him with us daily as he was growing up to teach him and encourage him to be his own person; to let him know all sides of us; to let him be an important part of our lives and us an important part of his.

June said, "But I'll have to have someone to travel with us who can help take care of John Carter so I can travel with you and perform."

I said, "We'll find somebody."

June said, "Just somebody won't do. It's got to be somebody really special, somebody who will really love him. A practicing Christian who'll help him bring out the best in himself."

I said, "Your prayers have a way of getting answered. Why don't you pray for that special someone?"

She was about to say, "I will," when into the room walked a beautiful, bright, smiling little nurse named Winafred Kelley. June introduced me to her, and she congratulated me on the boy and oohed and ahhed about how handsome he was. She puttered around the room arranging the flowers and puffing June up.

"Just my luck," said Mrs. Kelley, "to be off duty when John Carter was born. I've been here twenty years and had to miss the big one. Oh well. . . ." And she was gone.

I said, "If she's been here twenty years, maybe she's ready to leave this hospital."

June smiled and said, "I've had my eye on her."

A month later, Mrs. Kelley became a part of our family.

In April, 1970, we were booked for a performance

at the White House for the President and specially invited guests. Three days before the appearance, Reba called me.

"The President has requested three songs for your 'Evening at the White House' program," she said.

"You gotta be kidding," I replied. "Does he know my songs?"

"They aren't all yours," Reba said. "He wants *Boy Named Sue,* but he also requested *Welfare Cadillac* and *Okie From Muskogee.*"

There was a long pause on my end of the line. "You mean to say President Nixon requested those songs?"

"Well, I won't guarantee it, John," she said. "The actual request came from Bob Haldeman's office."

"Who is Bob Haldeman?" I asked.

"He's a presidential aide," she answered.

"Would you please call Mr. Haldeman," I said, "and tell him this for me: I appreciate the interest in my concert, I appreciate the request, and I will do *Boy Named Sue.*

"However, *Welfare Cadillac* is not something I could do," I continued. "I've only heard it once, and there's no time to learn it, even if I wanted to. *Okie From Muskogee* is Merle Haggard's song, and if they're inviting me to do a White House performance, I'm sure it won't be long till they ask Merle to do one. Let's just wait and let Merle do *Okie From Muskogee* for them himself."

Reba reported back to me later that Mr. Haldeman understood, and whatever I sang would be fine with the President.

In my mind the issue was resolved, but when I got to Washington all I heard was, "Johnny Cash has refused a presidential request!" A barrage of reporters surrounded me, asking about it.

"I didn't refuse a presidential request," I said. "I might have, *had there been one,* because I have my own reasons for not doing those two songs."

"What reasons?" a dozen people asked.

"I don't know *Welfare Cadillac,* and Merle Haggard sings *Okie From Muskogee.* I can't sing it like he can."

By show time, President Nixon himself had gotten word of my "refusal," and in his introduction of me he said in a lighthearted, joking way — ' **Johnny** Cash has brought his baby son, John Carter, and I understand he's asleep upstairs in the Lincoln bed. At the rate Johnny Cash is going, I'd say John Carter may be sleeping in my bed someday. . . .

"But about Johnny Cash's music — I realize now that I don't know it nearly as well as I should." (Laughter)

Then he concluded a nice introduction and nothing else was said about the songs I didn't do.

We did an hour concert, closing with gospel songs involving the whole group — Carl Perkins, the Tennessee Three, the Statlers, and the Carter Family. The audience, including the President, was warm and receptive. Then we formed a receiving line where we stood with the President meeting all the guests.

Later, the Nixons spent an hour with June and me, showing us the family quarters of the White House. They were warm, friendly, and talkative.

Afterwards in our motel, I asked June, "Did we ever meet Bob Haldeman?"

"Of course," she said. "He came through the receiving line."

"I wanted to thank him for those requests," I said. "Maybe I can do it later."

When we came back from Washington, John Carter developed a chest cold, and we had to take him back to Madison Hospital and put him in an oxygen tent for a couple of days. You're not allowed to smoke in that hospital, but I would go into the men's room and light up.

Then I'd go back in the room beside John Carter and lie down and start coughing. And every time I'd cough, it would wake him up and he'd cry. I could control my cough for awhile, but about the time he'd go back to sleep, I'd cough and he'd wake again.

Well, the next day Dr. Billy Burks, who is the husband of John Carter's pediatrician, came by with his wife who was checking John Carter. I was standing there coughing, and Dr. Burks looked me right in the eye and said, "Man, you need to quit smoking and you need to do it now."

"Yeah, I know it, Billy," I said, surprised at first by his frankness.

"You're going to kill yourself if you don't quit," he said.

"I know," I told him.

He said, "Well, we'll just help you quit smoking. Here at this hospital we have a clinic, a five-day-stop-smoking plan."

It began the next Monday night. It went Monday through Friday, two hours each night. The theme of the program is: "I choose not to smoke." The first hour each night is conducted by a doctor, the second hour by the chaplain, and it's really an eyeopener. They showed us medical films and gave us some commonsense talks and instructions on how to fight the craving for nicotine; they told us about foods and beverages to avoid which increase the desire to smoke.

By Friday night, April 23, 1970, I stopped smoking.

But talk about daily mountains! I'd smoked since I was a teen-ager, and it took thirty more days of prayer and fighting before the nicotine habit turned me loose.

I dreamed of cigarettes. I'd catch myself inhaling the fumes from the stove in the kitchen or looking at the leaves on the trees, wondering how they'd taste! After

three or four weeks, it began to get a little easier. Then I
felt the victory.

When the craving finally left me, so did the cough.

The songs and hymns I'd been singing since I was
a kid were brought into the format of the weekly TV
show. I sang all the ones I loved. The Carter Family, the
Statler Brothers, and Carl Perkins joined in on them, as
did June.

I enjoyed singing them with my "family" group.
Nobody ever had to learn the old songs. Every one of us
had known them all our lives.

Fans were writing letters asking millions of
personal questions, and among the questions being
asked now was, "Are you a Christian? It's apparent that
you have a church background, that you've sung gospel
songs, but are you a Christian?" I was anxious to answer
them — publicly.

Along about the middle of the second year on
television, on the way in from Hendersonville to
downtown Nashville where I taped the show at the Grand
Ole Opry House, June said, "What's the closing hymn
this week?" with a smile.

I said, "You know, June, it shouldn't be the
closing hymn. Why does every show have to have a
closing hymn? Why can't you find a place to spotlight a
song if you feel it's important to the show?"

And she said, "Well, if you feel it's important,
why don't you say it's important?"

I said, "That's a good idea. Why don't I say what
I'm really feeling. I don't own the network, but I'm going
to say what I feel on my show as long as I can pull it off."

When we arrived that day, the producers came to
me and said, "We need the introduction to the closing
hymn so we can put it on cue cards for you."

I said, "Don't want it on cue cards. Not this time.

I'd like to just do it off the top of my head, if you don't mind."

And they said, "Well, we really need to know exactly what you're going to say so we can get it timed out."

I said, "It's fifty seconds."

"Fine. You sure you don't want it on cue cards?"

"No, thank you," I replied.

The stage director said, "Okay, closing hymn. Take one. Five, four, three, two, one." And he threw the finger at me to start talking.

"Well, folks," I began, "I've introduced lots of hymns and gospel songs on this show. I just want to make it clear that I'm feeling what I'm singing about in this next one. I am a Christian.

"I've always known there are two powerful forces in this world — the forces of right and wrong, or the forces of good and bad. I choose to call it the force of God and the force of the devil.

"The number one power in this world is God. The number two power is Satan, and though he manages to fight for second in my life, I want to dedicate this song to the proposition that God is the victor in my life. I'd be nothing without Him. I want to get in a good lick right now for Number One."

And I sang *I Saw A Man.*

> Last night I dreamed an angel came.
> He took my hand; he called my name;
> He bid me look the other way.
> I saw a man; I heard him say.
>
> He said "If I be lifted up,
> I'll draw all men to me."
> He turned and then I saw,
> The nail-scarred hands that bled for me.
> I touched the hem of his garment
> That fell round him there.

My life, my heart I gave;
My soul was in his care.

When I awoke, my heart beat so,
And in the dark, I saw a glow.
This was no dream; he turned my way;
Again I heard my Savior say.

He said "If I be lifted up,
I'll draw all men to me."
He turned and then I saw,
The nail-scarred hands that bled for me.
I touched the hem of his garment
That fell round him there.
My life, my heart I gave;
My soul was in his care.

Words and Music by Arthur Smith, © 1954 Lynn Music Corp. Used by permission.

Well, at the end of the taping the producer came around to me and shook his head and said, "That's pretty heavy stuff you laid on them tonight, Cash."

I didn't even answer him. I just nodded my head, like, "Yeah, I know it."

Another part of the TV programs that I enjoyed was the "Ride This Train" segment. Merle Travis, Red Lane, Larry Murray, and I wrote these episodes. The idea came from an album I had recorded in 1959 by the same title. It was one of the first "concept" albums in our business.

Merle Travis had had an album called *Back Home* in which he talked and sang about life in the coal country of his native Kentucky. Some of his great compositions were in this album, such as *Dark as the Dungeon, Nine-Pound Hammer,* and *Sixteen Tons.*

In my second year on television I was greatly concerned that the show keep the honesty and realism in such things as "Ride This Train" that had contributed to its success in the first place.

Each week we took an imaginary train trip to some

time and place in the history of our country and relived in
song and story such Americana as the California Gold
Rush, the Pony Express days, the Old West, the Civil
War, the songs and career of Jimmy Rodgers and the Carter
Family, the Last Run of Casey Jones, and many more
exciting and interesting incidents in the history of our
country.

Through some great writing by Merle Travis, I
recounted the removal of the Cherokees under Andrew
Jackson, coal mining tales and songs, and the life of the
truck driver.

But a little too much outside influence from the
East Coast and the West Coast crept into the format of
the show. I found myself with a few guests with whom I had
nothing in common: cabaret and cafe society people
that I felt and looked out of place with. My audience knew it
also.

"Orders from headquarters" was the cop-out
answer I got when I questioned the reason for bringing
some of these people on my show.

Then they decided to cancel the "Ride This
Train" segment. That and the hymns were the only
things left I thought were really worthwhile.

"Tell headquarters I'm going to Australia," I told
my producers toward the end of the second season. "If I
can't keep in things of substance with truth and
down-to-earth dialogue like we've done in 'Ride This
Train,' if I can't choose my guests and most of them from
the country music community from here in Nashville,
and if I can't continue to do the shows from Nashville, tell
headquarters that it's just fine with June and me if the
TV show isn't renewed for next year."

Headquarters didn't renew.

Two of those last shows we did were really
noteworthy and personally rewarding. One was the
Campus Special, where our audience was the student body

of Vanderbilt University. I wrote a song for that concert
called *Man In Black*.

      Throughout the last few years whenever reporters
would get me cornered, they would always ask me how I
felt about social issues, problems, and prejudices. All these
reporters' questions were filed in the back of my mind
to be answered in this new song:

        Well, you wonder why I always dress in black,
        Why you never see bright colors on my back,
        And why does my appearance seem to have a
          somber tone.
        Well, there's a reason for the things that I have
          on.
        Ah, I wear the black for the poor and the
          beaten down,
        Livin' in the hopeless, hungry side of town,
        I wear the black for the prisoner who has long
          paid for his crime,
        But is there because he's a victim of the times.

        I wear the black for those who never read,
        Or listened to the words that Jesus said,
        About the road to happiness thru love and
          charity,
        Why, you'd think He's talking straight to you
          and me.
        Ah, we're doin' mighty fine, I do suppose,
        In our streak of lightnin' cars and fancy
          clothes,
        But just so we're reminded of the ones who
          are held back,
        Up front there ought 'a be a Man In Black.

        I wear it for the sick and lonely old,
        For the reckless ones whose bad trip left them
          cold,
        I wear the black in mournin' for the lives that
          could have been,
        Each week we lose a hundred fine young men.

Ah, I wear it for the thousands who have died,
Believin' that the Lord was on their side,
And I wear it for another hundred thousand
    who have died,
Believin' that we all were on their side.

Well, there's things that never will be right I
    know,
And things need changin' everywhere you go,
But until we start to make a move to make a
    few things right,
You'll never see me wear a suit of white.
Oh, I'd love to wear a rainbow every day,
And tell the world that everything's OK,
But I'll try to carry off a little darkness on my
    back,
Till things are brighter, I'm the Man In Black.

By John R. Cash, © 1971 House of Cash, Inc.

And even as I was writing the song, I tried, but couldn't find a place to put in the line, "Black is better for church."

The last TV show was the Gospel Music Special. We had the Oak Ridge Boys, the Blackwood Brothers, Mahalia Jackson, Stuart Hamblin, and Billy Graham.

The whole show was a closing hymn.

That was the spring of 1971, and we realized a chapter in our lives had come to a close. There had been some solid growth through the experience. Now it was time to move on.

17 / **Who Kept the Sheep?**

When we were taping the TV shows at the Grand
Ole Opry House in 1969 and '70, Rev. Jimmy Snow often
dropped by to see me. I had known Jimmy Snow since 1956
and had a lot of respect for him as a man, though I
hadn't heard him preach yet. I had seen him at his worst,
and he had seen me the same way later after he had been
converted and started preaching in the late fifties.

I felt comfortable around him, and conversation
was always easy with him. We had a common interest in
our music, for he had started out as a country singer before
his call to preach.

Now he had built and was pastoring a little church
out on Dickerson Road in Nashville — Evangel Temple.
The church had less than two hundred members, but he was
awfully proud of it.

"Why don't you come visit us sometime at the
church, John?" said Jimmy one night backstage at the
Opry House. "And bring your guitar and knock off a few
songs for us," he kidded.

"I thought you'd never ask," I said. "I'm not the
best one around for singing in church, but I'll try. When
do you want me?"

"Any time," he said. "How about Sunday night and bring your guitar?"

"You mean you allow guitars to be played in your church?" I asked.

"Guitars, banjos, electric bass, drums, piano, organ, trumpet, anything you're comfortable with," he said. "The 150th chapter of Psalms is still a part of my Bible."

"What's the 150th psalm got to do with it?" I asked.

"It tells you that you can bring your guitar to Evangel Temple," said Jimmy Snow. "See you Sunday night."

When I walked in the front door that next Sunday, just for a minute I was a little boy again. But there was no fear this time.

That fear had truly been the beginning of wisdom for me, for now I understood that these people were really worshiping. But there wasn't the frenzy I'd remembered. Instead, there was joy.

I stood silently and watched the congregation. They were singing softly. Some of their hands were raised, and their faces showed a quiet bliss. "This is the real thing," I felt. "An off-the-fence kind of worshiping." They weren't concerned with what the person in the next pew was thinking. It was true worship.

I found a seat on the side down near the front, set my guitar down, and stood with the congregation, savoring the rest of the song they were singing:

> There's a sweet, sweet spirit in this place,
> And I know that it's the Spirit of the Lord.
> There are sweet expressions on each face,
> And I know that it's the Spirit of the Lord.
> Sweet Holy Spirit, sweet heavenly dove,
> Stay right here with us,

Filling us with your love.
And for these blessings,
We lift our hearts in praise.
Without a doubt we know,
That we have been revived,
When we shall leave this place.

I looked around, and the familiar faces made me even more comfortable. Several people in the music business were there, and most of the ones I knew were people who had had a problem with drugs or liquor or some hard knocks of one kind or another, and they were all like brand-new.

Jimmy Snow called me up to sing, and for the first time I could ever remember I felt comfortable and enjoyed singing in church. There was no piano in the wrong key that I had to try to keep up with. I had my own guitar to do the choosing with, and I had chosen to sing a song I knew I'd be comfortable with — *My Prayer.*

When my way is light,
But I still can't see,
With a strong hand strike out,
The blindness in me,
Show me work that I should
Carry on for Thee,
Make my way straight and narrow,
Like you want it to be.

Lead me, Father, with your staff of life,
Give me strength for a song,
That the words I sing
Might more strength bring,
To help some poor troubled
Weary worker along.

When Jimmy started preaching, again it took me

back to my childhood for just a minute. I'd never known this Jimmy Snow before. He prayed at the beginning that he would remember every word he'd ever read that pertained to the topic of his sermon. He prayed for the conviction of unbelievers.

I think all his prayers were answered. His message was a simple, easy-to-understand sermon on the salvation of Jesus Christ, but I was amazed at his knowledge of the Bible.

"His mind is like a computer," I thought. "He can't keep those scriptures from rolling out one after the other even if he wants to."

As I was walking out of the church after the sermon, I looked back at the altar. Most of the congregation was on its knees at the altar, simply praying and worshiping. It seemed as though these people had looked forward to this moment in the service when they could go down and kneel in prayer and praise by those newly committed. Some were praying aloud, some silently. Some sat alone in their pews. Nobody was paying any attention to anyone else, including me, which I appreciated.

I didn't go back to Evangel Temple for many months, for I was always away on weekends doing concerts and taping the TV shows through the week. But I didn't forget the service and the spirit there. I knew I'd go back sometime.

By 1970, our daughter Rosey was attending church at Evangel Temple regularly, going and coming with her friends. She wanted June and me to take her, and we promised we would, and one Sunday near the end of 1970 we did.

"What did you think of the service?" I asked June afterwards.

"It reminded me of an old-fashioned service back home," she said.

We went back again, the third and the fourth time.

One Sunday in the spring of 1971 the service was especially inspiring. The church was packed, and expansion of the main auditorium was underway. My sister Joanne Yates was a member of the choir. I know she was glad to see me coming back there. The growth she had experienced in this place had been so apparent, and she wanted me to share it all.

The congregation sang a couple of rousing favorites like *At the Cross* and *Standing on the Promises*. This was one thing I loved about Evangel Temple. They hadn't gotten too fancy in their music and selection of songs. These hymns were the same ones I'd sung in church as a boy.

Then the choir sang a song. I had heard choirs before, but this one was different. They had on nice robes all right, and they filed in and took their places like ladies and gentlemen in church, but when they started singing, it was like something I'd never seen before. Some were snapping fingers, tapping toes, clapping hands, moving and swaying to the music. Their faces were like beacons. They had spirit, and the feeling was infectious. They were beautiful, and they sang like they believed it.

The guest singer for the day was a young man named Larry Gatlin. He sat on a stool beside the pulpit with his guitar, and without a word sang a song he had written called *Help Me*. I had never met Larry Gatlin and knew nothing about him at the time, except that I knew I'd never heard a better performance of any song by any artist at any time.

The whole audience sat spellbound while Larry sang:

> Come down from Your golden throne
> To me, lowly me,
> I need to feel the touch
> Of Your tender hand.

Remove the chains of darkness
And let me see, Lord, let me see,
Just where I fit into Your master plan.

I never thought I needed help before,
I thought that I could get by by myself,
Now I know I just can't make it any more,
With a humble heart on bended knees,
I'm begging You please, help me.

By Larry Gatlin, © First Generation Music. Used by permission.

"Can he know just how really true those words are?" I thought. "As young as he is, how lucky he is to know that he can't make it on his own." It had taken me a long time, and I bore many scars testifying to the fact that I had fought the idea from time to time that I couldn't make it by myself. How much suffering I could have saved myself and others over the years if I had rebuked and rejected Deception, Pride, Arrogance, and all the other demons from the time I was Gatlin's age and walked always with the Master.

But even as I thought on these things and Gatlin's song came to an end, I knew I would not look back in regret. Some burned bridges could not be rebuilt. The future was the important thing now. What I did with my life from now on was all that mattered. I had learned a lot from my mistakes, and I'd learned the tempering, steeling hard way.

Jimmy's message was powerful. I had gotten used to his style and to him and let myself be "fed." He touched on great spiritual truths and explained them in a way a child could understand.

I had learned to really love the Word through my father-in-law, Ezra Carter. I had seen that same enthusiasm in him many times when we were in one of our long historical and theological discussion sessions.

I remembered Pop Carter jumping up and

excitedly grabbing a commentary by nineteenth century theologian Lange.

"Who kept the sheep?" Pop had quizzed me.

"What sheep, Pop?" I asked.

"The sheep that the shepherds abandoned when they went to see the newborn Christ in Bethlehem," Pop said excitedly.

"I don't know," I said after a minute. "Who kept the sheep, Pop?"

"Nobody did," said Pop quietly, with a smile. "Those sheep were being reared on choice pasture to be presented without blemish for a sacrifice on the altar at Jerusalem. Don't you see, John?" he continued. "With the newborn Lamb of God born in Bethlehem to be sacrificed for the sins of man, being the one and only blood sacrifice needed for man, the old sacrifices could be abandoned. *Nobody* kept the sheep!"

I had seen and shared the joy of that and many other great truths with Pop Carter. Pop was not an active church member, but he was a better Christian on Monday than he was on Sunday.

Now Jimmy Snow was closing the service. He made an appeal to "believers" as well as "nonbelievers" to make a commitment to Christ, to "get off the fence with your faith," to make a public stand, "if you really mean it."

The invitation continued for several minutes. I thought of the time when I was twelve when I had gone to the altar, when I had made my original decision. Twenty-seven years had gone by. I had learned the long-suffering and complete forgiveness of God. What a joy to know that He'd clean the slate for all those years.

"I'm reaffirming my faith," I told Jimmy Snow. "I'll make the stand, and in case I've had any reservations up to now, I pledge that I'm going to try harder to live my life as God wants, and I'd like to ask your prayers and the prayers of these people."

In the weeks that followed, June and I discussed church membership. "I was brought up a Methodist," she said. "I'm not sure I believe everything the way they do at Evangel Temple."

"I was brought up a Baptist," I said, "and I'm not sure I agree with their doctrine either, but on the other hand, I'm not sure that it's even important to me."

We discussed the possible disadvantages, as entertainers, of belonging to a particular denomination. "If we're going to start nit-picking on what's right or what's wrong with this or that church, we could soon forget what we need a church home for in the first place," I said. "I need a spiritual foundation here on the earth that we have to walk around on. I need a spiritual anchor that I can reach back and grab hold of when I begin to drift. I'm human, and I need all the help I can get.

"I never thought church membership would be important to me," I said. "Of course, it isn't as important as believing, and you can worship God anywhere, but I need everything He has to offer to give me support and courage.

"I've made 'commitments' before," I said. "I depended only on myself and what little wisdom I had to make it stick, and it didn't work out. I'm not playing church. I'm dead serious this time."

When I shook Jimmy Snow's hand, I didn't mean that I agree with every little thing his church teaches. I wasn't talking about doctrine.

"What I did mean," I said, "was that I'm serious about wanting to live right. What I did mean was that I believe in Jesus Christ, and I want to follow Him and know Him better. And I did mean that I need Jimmy's and the congregation's prayers to help me know how to cope with the temptations and vices that are always with me. More than that, in asking for their prayers I am admitting that I can't handle it all by myself. We saw what happened when I tried that way. I mean I'm serious about God. That's what I mean.

"Other than that," I said, "I just naturally feel good at a service with the bunch of would-be down-and-outers and losers you see in that congregation.

"There's Larry Lee, who works for us at House of Cash. He must have taken a trainload of dope in his day, and there he sits up by the piano, smiling and playing rhythm guitar. And there must be two dozen more with a past like mine and Larry Lee's. Several musicians and music business people who've had some awfully hard knocks, but who're happy with a new life found there.

"Yes, I think I'll join Evangel Temple," I said. "There's just enough underdogs and second-lifers over there to make me comfortable — my sister Joanne for one. I've got a lot in common with them. They understand me."

By the time Sunday morning came around, June had decided on her own to join the church with me.

18 / **Gospel Road**

There comes a time in every man's life when he realizes the need to try to accomplish one thing that will say to the world, "This is the best I had to offer. This is me. This is what I'd like my life to say."

That moment came for June and me in the production of a movie called *Gospel Road,* our story of Jesus told and sung. A movie designed to be entertaining, carrying the identification mark of my music, but a movie that is an expression of our faith: our witness and testimony and the overshadowing power in it to be the words of Jesus.

At least one national sponsor expressed interest in the project for a television special, but insisted on seeing a screenplay for network approval.

"There is no screenplay," I said. "This is one film that cannot follow according to network script approval. This film is going to be an extension of ourselves — an expression of our faith, told however we feel it when the cameras start to roll."

We were happy to see that this national sponsor lost interest for the time being. Now we could proceed with what we wanted to do and had to do: step out on faith, don't count the cost, and see it through.

June and I had been to Israel twice before, and it was like going home. The first time we were there, June had come to me the first morning at the King David Hotel in Jerusalem and said, "Last night I had a dream. I saw you on a mountaintop in Israel, and you had a book in your hand — maybe it was a Bible — and you were talking to millions of people about Jesus."

That scared me a little because I wasn't ready yet for any such thing. I knew that I wasn't physically and spiritually able for such a role.

We got to talking and decided maybe it was a record we were supposed to do. But we didn't take the matter lightly because the visionlike dream had made such a strong impression on June.

A few days later when we got to Galilee, the land where Jesus had lived, June tugged my sleeve and said, "There's the mountain I dreamed about where you were standing."

I said, "Well, it must be something else besides a record."

We had gone back to Israel in 1968 and recorded the album *Johnny Cash in the Holy Land.* And we did tell a story of Jesus in that music. But it wasn't all there — something was missing. June saw the album cover and said, "That wasn't my dream."

The missing element was the vision. Because as time went by, we saw more and more clearly the thing we had to do.

The dream had come at a time when I was beginning to decide to live. By 1969 I was gaining strength again, but had my two-year television series to keep me busy. But by 1971 I was not only free timewise to make the film, but I thought I had learned a few things to tell about Jesus.

I studied and prepared myself for the job of telling with authority the story of Jesus.

I talked to people in all walks of religious life. I talked to Jews. I hungered for a broader understanding of the Chosen People and found their faith as diversified as Christian denominations.

On a plane in Sweden I talked with a professor of political science from Yashiva University in New York. I told him about the plans for the movie. And he told me much about the daily lives of the people of Palestine during the time of Christ that gave me insight into the historical period of my interest. He also gave me names of people in the Israeli government who would help us with the project.

"A most illustrious man was your Jesus," said the professor.

"But what do you mean, 'illustrious'?" I asked.

He laughed. "He has His name on churches and buildings all over the world; more than any man who ever lived, I suppose."

"Professor, believe me," I said, "He wouldn't want His name on some of those churches."

"Why wouldn't He?" he asked.

"Jesus claimed to be the Son of God, the Messiah," I said. "He allowed Himself to be killed as a sacrifice for all mankind's sins, and to prove His divinity He arose from the dead.

"The reason He wouldn't want His name on some churches is that some of them reduce Him to a mere prophet or a philosophizing do-gooder, denying His divinity. I have more tolerance for people of other religions who traditionally reject the divinity of Jesus than I do for those people who claim to be Christians, yet disclaim and deny His virgin birth, His resurrection, or any of His miracles."

"Many Jews consider Him a prophet," said the professor, "and a very wise man."

The plane was landing in Stockholm.

"He was that, sir," I said. "But much more."

"Good luck on your project," said the professor. "You'll love Israel."

We toured Sweden, Germany, Denmark, Norway, and England doing concerts. Back in the hotel, every night into the early hours of the morning I studied the Bible and a "Harmony of the Gospels" which laid out the life of Christ in chronological order as best it can be done.

At Foyle's bookshop in London I bought an armload of "Life of Christ" by various writers.

The first one I opened was a nineteenth century theologian named Fleetwood. I turned the pages at random, and the first thing I read was:

> Let every man who commits his thoughts
> to the public take special care that nothing
> drop even incidental from his pen that can
> offend those who profess to believe in the
> Savior, so as to either stagger their faith or
> corrupt their hearts.

I read much of Fleetwood, always checking him against the Bible. I read Stalker, Lange, and others.

Some others I threw in the trash can at the first indication of serious lack of faith in the writer. One book which called a particular incident in the life of Christ "a traditional legend" I threw out the window onto the top of another building. "Boy," I thought, "the Bible *does* shed a lot of light on commentaries."

Back home I had long talks with Pop Carter and with June.

"The songs you sing in the film are going to be awfully important," said June. "Songs that help tell the story. For instance, the visualization of Jesus carrying the cross, and the crucifixion, must be good, but with you singing a song through the scene that brings home the emotion and power of it all, it should have a convicting impact."

"It will," said Pop. "I always knew you had a special purpose in this life, and this is it."

"I'll do my best, Pop," I said.

"Just let Him guide you," he said.

Robert Elfstrom, a fine documentary film maker, was hired to direct the project. He also portrayed Christ. An Israeli film company was hired to supplement Elfstrom's crew of technicians.

In all we took about thirty people to Israel, including Jimmy Snow, Larry Lee, Larry Butler, who was my record producer at the time, my secretary, Mr. and Mrs. Kelley, John Carter, and Rosey.

Exhausted from the trip, we arrived at the hotel in Tiberias overlooking the Sea of Galilee. John Carter had a fever from a cold he'd caught on the plane. I looked out the window at the moonlit Sea of Galilee through tired, bloodshot eyes.

"What a mountain we've chosen to climb this time," I told June. "Where did we ever get the idea we know anything about producing a movie?"

"Well," she said sleepily, "let's don't call it a movie. Let's call it our 'testimony.' We know how to do that."

"Yeah," I said. "And it begins five hours from now at 4:00 A.M., in order to be out on the north end of Galilee to start shooting at sunup."

"Good night," I said, but June was already asleep.

I peeped in on the Kelleys. They were on their knees praying for sunup tomorrow.

June was there with me everyday behind the camera: encouraging, criticizing, and complimenting. I bounced a lot of ideas off her. Some of her own suggestions I rejected, but most of them were put into action.

June had had two years of dramatic training at the Neighborhood Playhouse in New York in the fifties, and her professional capabilities are evident in her portrayal of Mary Magdalene. She played a five-minute scene that is the emotional peak of the show: the cleansing of Mary Magdalene.

My sister Reba worked at any and every job she could see needed doing. Reba is one of those rare people who gets the job done before you can tell her it needs doing. Those childhood years she and I shared, the hard work we did together, had established a bond of love and understanding which works well today. She took on *Gospel Road* as a personal challenge and put her heart and soul into seeing it through.

For thirty days we followed our hearts and a rough outline on the life of Christ, which I'd prepared with the help of Larry Murray who'd been a writer on my TV shows.

Thirty days of shooting went off without a hitch. The Israeli government cleared locations for us, and the army provided security and escorted us to many locations around Jericho, the desert around the Dead Sea, the Jordan Valley, the Wilderness of Judea, Nazareth, Cana, the ruins at Capernaum, and other actual sites for the scenes in the life of Christ.

One of our drivers was an Arab from Jericho. He had a hard time at first getting along with the Israeli drivers, but being greatly outnumbered he took the cold shoulder from them with a smile. He proved to be a valuable man in the production, arranging for permission for us to shoot in some predominantely Arab populated areas.

My favorite location, and one where I spent many hours alone, was a mountaintop, Mt. Arabel, above Tiberias and overlooking Galilee. From there I could see Mt. Hermon, Mt. Tabor, the Horns of Hattin, and the whole of the Sea of Galilee.

I would go there between locations or between scenes, sit on a rock, and seek my directions. I felt good there. Like many other places where I felt His presence, I felt that Jesus had sat on the same rock, looking out across that same sea; or more likely He had kneeled by that same rock for some of His long talks with the Father.

"Then," I said to myself, "maybe He stood here with His disciples around Him, teaching them."

"Teach me, too," I whispered. "The more I learn of You, the more I realize I don't know."

But I told that camera and recorder everything I knew, everything I felt.

Elfstrom and the capable cast played out the roles of the people in the incidents I related: the baptism of Jesus by John the Baptist, the descent of the dove — a symbol of the Spirit, the miracle at Cana — turning the water into wine, the meeting with Nicodemus, the healing of a blind man, the forgiving of a woman caught in adultery, the cleansing of the temple, the confrontation of scribes and pharisees, and many, many more events down through the crucifixion and resurrection and ascension of Christ.

We came home at the end of November feeling that our mission was accomplished, but the really tough job was just beginning.

The film was taken to an editing room in New York City where nine months were spent making it work. During that time, songs were written and recorded to help tell the story, and the songs and my narration were slowly, carefully added to the film.

Harold and Don Reid of the Statler Brothers wrote *Lord, Is It I* for the film, and the Statlers sing it on the sound track.

This was one of the last projects the Statler Brothers took part in with me, because about this time, having been with me for eight years as featured vocalists on my show, we mutually agreed it was time they headline their own show.

And how right we were! The trade magazines, the fans, and the music industry voted them the number one vocal group in our business, and they won more top record and top group awards than we could count. They have become an American tradition, singing songs of mother, home, country, and God. The Statlers are the kind of stuff this country is made of, and I'm proud that I might have had a small part in seeing them become established.

Their annual "Happy Birthday USA" celebration on July 4th in their hometown of Staunton, Virginia, draws 50,000 to 100,000 every year.

And, by the way, one of the greatest times of my life was at their second annual "Happy Birthday," when I was their guest in Staunton. People came for hundreds of miles, dinners in their picnic baskets, and country and gospel music happened all day and all night. And the highlight of the day for me was to again get to see and hear the Statler Brothers perform. They were better there that day in Staunton than I had ever seen them.

When the celebration ended, Harold Reid and I had some time to talk.

"How does our song *Lord, Is It I* work in *Gospel Road?*" he asked.

"Beautifully," I said. "It sets the whole scene for the Last Supper."

"Hope it makes them want a box of popcorn when they hear it in the movie," Harold said.

"Why is that?" I asked.

"Because the more popcorn they eat, the better you know the movie is," he answered.

Our movie was still a long way from "selling any popcorn"!

Kris Kristofferson came to see a "rough-cut" version of *Gospel Road* in New York.

We had already decided to use Larry Gatlin's *Help Me,* plus another song he wrote especially for us called *Last Supper.*

Prior to viewing the movie, Kris visited June and me in our hotel room and sang us two songs he had just written.

"I went to your church in Nashville awhile back," Kris said.

"My church? You mean Evangel Temple?"

"Yeah," he said, "and I don't understand much about what happened. That preacher, Snow, asked if anybody felt guilty and needed Jesus they should raise their hand."

"And you raised your hand?" I asked.

"Well, yeah," he said. "I mean, man, I feel guilty about the *weather.* And I figured that if Jesus had everything to offer that Snow said He did, everybody needed some of that."

"And then he asked you to come down to the altar, right?" I asked.

"Well, yeah," he said, "but what I was getting to is that I wrote a couple of Jesus songs afterwards, and I never thought I'd do any such thing."

"Sing them for us," I said.

"Do you know Larry Gatlin?" Kris asked.

"Very well," I said.

"Well, one of the songs I wrote is called *Why Me, Lord?* Gatlin sang *Help Me* at church when I was there, and it about killed me. Then Snow started talking about Jesus and how He loved me no matter if I am a rotten so-and-so, and I just had to write one called *Why Me, Lord?*

Why me, Lord?
What have I ever done
To deserve even one

> Of the pleasures I've known?
> Tell me, Lord,
> What did I ever do
> That was worth loving you
> Or the kindness you've shown?
>
> By Kris Kristofferson, © 1972 Resaca Music. Used by permission.

"It's beautiful," June said when he finished. "Sing the other one."

Kris sang *Burden of Freedom,* and throughout the song I could see Jesus carrying His cross, falling, struggling, making the long, torturous journey to Calvary.

> Lord, help me to shoulder
> This Burden of Freedom,
> And give me the courage
> To be what I am.
> And when I am wounded,
> By those who condemn me,
> Father, forgive them,
> They don't understand.
>
> By Kris Kristofferson, © 1967 Buckhorn Music Publishers, Inc. Used by permission. All rights reserved.

Burden of Freedom was used in *Gospel Road. Why Me, Lord?* was recorded by Kris and his wife, Rita, and has become a gospel classic.

By the time we were ready to show the film to agents and distributors, it was 1973, and the news and publicity that had gone out on the project had generated a little interest in Hollywood.

One day we found ourselves showing *Gospel Road* in the theater at 20th Century Fox studios to a couple of hundred interested agents, distributors, and movie exhibitors, and later found ourselves with an offer from Fox to distribute *Gospel Road.*

"But we've never had a film like this, and we don't know how to market it," they confessed.

"I'll help," I said.

With Marshall Grant making the arrangements and traveling with me, and sometimes with June, sometimes with my daughter Rosanne, sometimes with John Carter and the whole show group, I crisscrossed the country for weeks and months, squeezing personal appearances at movie openings and premieres in-between my concerts.

Just when I thought I'd reached the last valley with *Gospel Road,* there was another new mountain. I was advised by some to forget it and let 20th Century Fox do the work. But I had a year and half of my life and the whole of my heart tied up in this project, and to me the battle was just getting interesting.

I looked at my schedule for 1973 and talked it over with Marshall.

"Every day of the year is filled," I told him. "Look at my calendar."

The days booked for concerts were in black, the days booked for movie openings where I'd make a personal appearance and introduce the film to the audience were marked in red.

"I'll go with you on every one of them, John," said Marshall. "If you can make it, I can. But it looks to me like you've got more requests from 20th Century Fox for appearances than you have days left, and it's costing you a fortune."

"Some of the black x's on my calendar will have to be changed to red," I said.

So like a whirlwind Marshall and I hit Indianapolis, Grand Rapids, Charlotte, Atlanta, Memphis, Denver, Seattle, New York City, San Antonio, Dallas, San Diego, San Jose, Jackson, Mississippi, and many, many more. Sometimes I'd barely make the theater on time.

"There comes a time in every man's life. . . ," I'd begin, and I'd do a song or two, and they'd see *Gospel*

Road. Receptions, picture taking, handshaking. Theaters were nearly always full.

June and I invited Billy and Ruth Graham to our home to see the movie.

"We've never distributed a film that we didn't produce ourselves," said Billy. "But World Wide Pictures must distribute *Gospel Road*. We know its audience."

Billy went from there to Chicago, and a meeting was held to screen *Gospel Road* for his organization. The vote was unanimous that negotiations be made with Fox to obtain distribution rights to *Gospel Road,* and the deal was made.

Our film was an instant success through World Wide, with hundreds of prints showing to packed churches every week, week after week, year round. Many hundreds have made a commitment to Christ upon Billy Graham's filmed invitation at the end of the picture.

World Wide Pictures has dubbed the film for Spanish-speaking countries and has asked me to record all the songs in Spanish, with an assistant who speaks Spanish working with me at the session teaching me to sing the songs phonetically.

I said, jokingly, "What about German, French, Italian, and Scandinavian?"

They answered seriously, "And Japanese and Chinese and maybe someday Russian."

Lately I've thought, "The more mountains I'm climbing, the more I enjoy the view from the top."

My old friend Rev. Floyd Gressett retired from his ministry at Avenue Community Church in Ventura, and for over a year, covering the time *Gospel Road* was controlled by 20th Century Fox, he took a print of *Gospel Road* as a labor of love and screened it in every prison and jail in the United States where they would allow him to do so.

He estimated that over 150,000 prisoners from New York to California saw our story of Jesus.

Many hundreds made a commitment to Christ upon Rev. Gressett's invitation at the end, and I have received hundreds of letters from prisoners who saw it and wrote to say "thanks."

So the dream came true — June's visionary dream back in 1966 — a dream that in coming true came about by divine direction. Of that, June and I have no doubt. And it all came true — because *Gospel Road* does open on a mountaintop in Israel, I have a Bible in my hand, and I'm talking about Jesus.

19 / **Old Gray Whiskers**

I have learned that a Christian cannot perform a totally secular concert. If I'm singing *A Boy Named Sue,* or *Folsom Prison Blues,* or *Precious Memories* I feel the same strength. I enjoy the traveling, the backstage waiting, and have even gotten used to the stale coffee we get in some hotels and dressing rooms.

I know that I must try to let a good light shine and try to live my daily life with charity and tolerance for those whose lives I touch, whether they be saint or sinner.

Tolerance — yes. Compromise — no.

How well I have learned that there is no fence to sit on between heaven and hell. There is a deep, wide gulf, a chasm, and in that chasm is no place for any man. And I must pity those who say they don't believe in God. Even the devil believes in God.

What an obligation Christians have to those who are seeking — even to nonbelievers who are not seeking; and the entertainment world is the front line for spiritual battles. But the success formula for pulling it off is simple. As Sonny James said in 1955, "I make it by being what I am."

I feel as at ease talking to a fellow entertainer who is half-drunk as I do discussing theology with Pat Boone. I can take my family to dinner at McDonald's or a nightclub and enjoy the meal.

Once a Christian puts himself above the world, or in his fervor becomes "holier than thou" or too good to associate with people of questionable character, then he has alienated the very people who need what he has to share, which is why I wrote —

> Come hear me, good brothers,
> Come hear one and all,
> Don't brag about standing,
> Or you'll surely fall.
> You're shining your light,
> Yes, and shine it you should,
> But you're so heavenly minded,
> You're No Earthly Good.
>
> If you're holding heaven,
> Then spread it around,
> There are hungry hands reaching,
> To you from the ground.
>
> You could give a drink,
> From your well if you would,
> But you're so heavenly minded,
> You're No Earthly Good.
>
> Come hear me, good sisters,
> You salt of the earth,
> If your salt isn't salty,
> What is its worth?
> Help someone to share,
> The high ground where you stood,
> So heavenly minded,
> You're No Earthly Good.
>
> By John R. Cash, © 1974 House of Cash, Inc.

I remember well the lesson I learned from the busted britches. I am not so sure of myself that I think

I'm too strong to fall. I know that I can't always, and won't always, resist every temptation. I know the dangers of walking through dark valleys, and when I do so, the Shepherd is never too far away.

I know how easily I can be influenced by my environment. I expect to make some wrong decisions in my personal and professional life, as I have many times before, but I expect to do better as I grow.

Satan always has a new trick to use. He is the great imitator, the great counterfeiter, and he can make anything look beautiful and right. In seeing through his imitations, in acknowledging my mistakes and short-comings, in denouncing, rebuking, and rejecting what I sincerely believe is wrong for me — based upon what little heavenly wisdom I have gleaned, and in daily contact with the Counselor — I get a better definition of what really is beautiful and right.

My baptism in and communion with the Holy Spirit has not been that unique spiritual ecstasy I have seen other people experience, but He's always with me.

I go for days, weeks without thinking of a pill; then in a moment of tension or anger, there's that old gnawing again, a craving for the old poison. Usually I fight it off and pray it off in just a minute's time. But each time is a reminder that the demons are never going to give up, so I know that I've got to possess all the tools of the trade to keep the ship on course. And the Carpenter is showing me how to use some of His tools.

He and I have established a line of communication — a kind of bond, and the bond has stood many tests and trials. He and I both know that many more trials will come, but He makes me know that because I am truly committed, that I profess Him and let Him know I need Him, He won't let me slip too low or slide too far before He grabs hold again.

For example, an incident that happened on Labor

Day, 1974, made me slow down in my work, which I was
engaged in at a killing pace. This event was a testing and
trying time for me. It seemed every day and every hour of my
life were taken up by work, concerts, recordings, TV
specials, appearances for this or that cause, day after day,
week after week, until I felt I was being spread a little thin.

I even found myself dreading some of the things on
my schedule, till finally on Labor Day I had to cancel a
TV appearance, being exhausted physically and mentally.
June and I had gone to Bon Aqua, our farm an hour west
of Nashville, to rest up for a few days. It was there we
received the call that John Carter and several other children
were at the hospital as the result of an accident.

My sister Reba had been driving my jeep with the
top off, loaded down with children — John Carter, his
cousins and friends, eight in all.

They drove all over the fields and woods. Then on
the road near my house the front wheels hit loose gravel,
and the jeep turned completely over with John Carter and
his cousin Kevin Jones under it. A Grand Ole Opry tour
bus bringing fans out our way was just behind the jeep
before it turned over. The bus stopped, and the people
poured off the bus and turned the jeep over immediately.

John Carter and Kevin had minor cuts that had
bled, and I'm sure it was a terrible looking scene with the
mud and the blood, so the first report I got by phone was
gloomy.

I was told that the children had been taken to
Madison Hospital, and when June and I arrived there an
hour and a half later, my parents and several friends and
relatives were waiting for us in the emergency room.

It seemed like an eternity before anyone would tell
us anything. Finally my daddy said, "They took John
Carter to Vanderbilt Children's Hospital." We couldn't
ask his condition. My knees trembled, June collapsed
on the floor, and just when I thought I couldn't live to face

any bad news we might hear after a thirty-minute drive
to Vanderbilt, I felt a pair of strong arms around me and a
familiar voice saying, "Just thank God he's alive. Let's
go to Vanderbilt."

I turned around to face Roy Orbison. My old
friend had come running at the news of the accident.

Roy had lost his first wife in a motorcycle
accident; then not long afterward his house burned and
two of his three little boys had died in the fire.

Roy's wife, Barbara, had her arms around June,
leading her to the car.

"And thank God for sending you at a time like this,
Roy Orbison," I cried.

Roy and Barbara encouraged us and gave us
strength to get out of the car and run into emergency
when we reached Vanderbilt.

Then we heard John Carter cry. Roy Orbison
jumped up and down. "Listen to him cry! Listen to
that!" he yelled. "Fantastic! Fantastic!"

We burst into the operating room, and the doctor
gave us the news we had prayed for.

"Well, it isn't as serious as we thought at first," he
said. "As you can hear, he's awake now and the x-rays
show only a concussion and possibly a small skull fracture.
These little ones have a way of bouncing back quickly."

They took John to intensive care, where he
would stay for a day to make sure he had no
further complications.

I walked into the waiting room, and there sat
Kristofferson, Larry Gatlin, and Vince Matthews.

"I checked him in for you," said Kris. "I guess I
caused an uproar in that admitting office. I couldn't
remember if his birthday was March 2nd or March 3rd. I
asked that girl what difference does it make?"

"I appreciate you guys coming," I said.

"We beat the ambulance here," said Vince.
"Heard it on the radio, so we ran over."

"One of those nurses has Gatlin's Mickey Mouse wristwatch," said Kris.

I was thinking of John Carter and was having a hard time following the conversation. June was down the hall standing at the door of the Intensive Care Unit.

"What did you say about Gatlin's Mickey Mouse watch?" I asked.

"The nurse down there has it," said Kris. "She borrowed it to check John Carter's pulse beat because it has a second hand."

"I'll get it back for you," I said to Gatlin.

"You can have it if you want it," said Gatlin.

"I want it," I said. "I want to wear it from now on as a reminder that a miracle was worked here today."

"John Carter would be glad to hear that old Mickey Mouse was his doctor," said Kris.

"Are you really going to wear it?" Vince asked me.

"Till it falls to pieces," I said.

"Johnny Cash with a Mickey Mouse watch," said Kris. "There goes your he-man image."

The other children were discharged, and for the three days we kept John Carter in the hospital for observation I did a lot of thanksgiving and soul-searching.

I must slow down. I must keep priorities in order. I must weed out the commitments I make that are not a part of what I feel He really wants me to do.

And I must find time to take my little boy fishing any time it's really important to him.

Rosanne had stayed at the hospital all night that first night we were there; then seeing that John Carter was going to be all right, she and Kathy had left with the church group for Israel.

Rosanne had sat in the waiting room with her Bible in her lap, a well-read, dog-eared Bible. She had been terrified at the news of the accident and had clutched her

Bible and prayed. She still clutched it in victory when she realized that prayers had been answered.

I hadn't said anything to her or anyone else after Kris, Vince, and Gatlin left. I was recharting my life's direction. But in my meditation I thought of Rosanne, of Rosey, Carlene, Kathleen, Cindy, and Tara. What happiness they gave June and me, being Christians in a time and in a world where it isn't especially popular to be one.

June had recently received a much-deserved award which bore testimony to the valuable role she and her influence and instruction had played in some of our girls' lives. Youth for Christ International had honored her at a surprise banquet in San Diego and named her "Wife and Mother of the Year 1974."

Rosanne, Carlene, Rosey, John Carter, and I had been there to help spring the surprise on her.

Rosanne graduated from high school in Ventura in 1973, and since that time has lived with us in Hendersonville, working with us in concert, as has Rosey. Kathleen, now eighteen, moved to Tennessee from California and has joined our staff at the House of Cash.

Carlene had performed with us until her marriage to singer-writer Jack Ruth, a talented young man whom we believe has a fine future in the music industry. He has recently signed a recording contract with RCA Victor.

June had said many times, "All six of our girls are going to be all right. I have committed them to God."

The third and last night in the hospital with John Carter, I picked up the Gideon Bible and turned to a verse of Scripture that said exactly what I felt.

> *I have no greater joy than to hear that my children walk in truth* (3 John, verse 4).

I took a pen and a get-well card that had come to John Carter and wrote the song in a few minutes.

I prayed for greater joy in my salvation,
A selfish prayer I finally came to know,
For the greatest joy while living comes to me
    when I am giving,
Giving children bread of life and watching
    them grow.

And my greatest joy is knowing that my
    children walk in truth,
And that they are giving You, Lord, of their fire
    and strength of youth.

Yes, I found that the joy of my salvation,
Is knowing that my children walk in truth.

By John R. Cash, © 1974 House of Cash, Inc.

In January 1975 still another parallel between
Carl Perkins's and my life occurred. His father passed away
after a lengthy illness, but June and I were unable to attend
the funeral because on the same day we were at another
funeral — that of my father-in-law, Ezra J. Carter.

Jimmy Snow told the congregation how God's
Word had always been Ezra Carter's sword, his shield, and
his comfort; how he could not and would not let go of that
sword all of his life.

"All of you who knew and loved this man —
remember that he didn't pass through your life
accidentally," Jimmy Snow said. "This was a man of God,
and if his life touched yours, it was for a purpose."

Pop Carter had suffered three heart attacks
and a stroke in the months before death came. His
hospitalization had been long and painful, though he found
much comfort in his family. Mother Maybelle never left his
side. Helen and her husband, Glen Jones, practically *lived*
at the hospital for five months, and she read to Pop from the
Bible when he no longer was able to talk, but still
could listen.

Knowing how he loved the Old Testament
prophets, I often read him those portions — especially

Isaiah. He found so much peace in Isaiah 53, which tells of the suffering Messiah.

"Ezra Carter's mind has been on heavenly things for years," Jimmy Snow was saying. "He was prepared. He was ready for the rewards which he had long studied about and worked for."

I listened to Jimmy preach, yet I couldn't stop my mind from wandering back to the many hours Pop and I had spent together on so many occasions. He not only had loved and appreciated the richness of the Bible, but had also marveled at its many mysteries and curiosities.

"Did you know that Moses was a singer?" Pop had quizzed me once.

"Really?" I kidded him. "What record company was he with?"

"No, seriously," Pop said. "The first verse of the fifteenth chapter of Exodus says, 'Then sang Moses and the children of Israel this song unto the Lord, and spake, saying, 'I will sing unto the Lord, for he hath triumphed gloriously: the horse and his rider hath he thrown into the sea.' "

Pop left me his complete library of biblical and historical books, a priceless collection of many complete volume sets of commentaries, Bibles, biblical study books, geographical and archaeological references, and even some of the little-known writings of the early church fathers of the second and third centuries. It is a library he spent a lifetime building.

But the greatest thing he left was the memory of himself. I loved even his human failings. Like, he had no patience for people who took up his time with petty plans or petty complaints. He was a hard worker and had nothing in common with people who weren't.

He had a temper. He had such a feeling for justice, for right and wrong, that he would throw a tantrum and read with rage of a burglary or a political scandal. Everything was either black or white for him; there were no gray areas.

Carl Perkins had missed a few tours with us, having taken care of his father during his illness. So when we began a tour of one-night stands from Florida to Maine in late February of 1975, we were all glad to be back on the road and to have Carl with us.

Jerry Hensley, a fine singer and musician, had taken Carl's place during his absence. But Jerry had fit in so well and was so well-liked, that everyone wanted him to stay on — even with Carl back. So Jerry Hensley became part of our musical family.

Las Vegas, Nevada, April of 1975 — We were back in Vegas for the first of three ten-day appearances scheduled at the Hilton Hotel for 1975. The Oak Ridge Boys, a gospel singing group, were back with us there for the third time.

Dozens of letters had come to the dressing room from people who came as a family to the concerts in the Hilton Showroom thanking us for a "clean" show. We do the same program in Vegas that we do anywhere, even though we realize that audiences there are not exactly the "state fair" variety.

On the eleventh and final night of our engagement, I stood backstage with Gordon Terry while the Oak Ridge Boys sang *The Baptism of Jesse Taylor*.

They baptized Jesse Taylor in
   Cedar Creek last Sunday.
Jesus gained a soul and Satan lost a
   good right arm.
They all cried "Hallelujah,"
   when Jesse's head went under,
'Cause this time he went under
   for the Lord!

It was midnight, and we were beginning our twenty-second show for this engagement, two a night at 8:00 and 12:00.

At 8:00 it was a dinner show, and the audience was usually a little more reserved, but enthusiastic and receptive. Some of them were long-time fans — people who had followed us for years and knew and appreciated what we did.

The midnight crowd was somewhat different. They *really* came to enjoy themselves — and if they decided to enjoy me, too, then all the better. There were men and women, drinkers, gamblers, midnight ramblers — people who catch all the shows in town, from the nudes to the dudes.

I've always loved the challenge of "getting through" to the audience at the Hilton. The showroom itself is probably the finest I've ever performed in, with near-perfect acoustics and lighting. It seats 3,000.

Gordon and I peeped through the curtains, sizing up the crowd.

"Not exactly the Oak Ridge Boys' hometown fan club gathered out there tonight," Gordon said.

"Not exactly mine either," I said. "But with twenty-one shows down and one to go, I'm going to enjoy it."

Gordon would go on next in about five minutes.

"How are you making it in Las Vegas, Gordon?" I asked.

He knew exactly what I meant. It had been thirteen months now since he had given his life over to Christ.

"With everything here that the spiritually dead world has to offer," he replied, "I stay in my room all the time except to go eat. I read my Bible some, but you know, it's hard to concentrate on that Bible around here."

There was a lot of truth in what he said. And I knew it was difficult for him being alone most of the time. Even though I had my family along in the fine accommodations the hotel provided, still — with two concerts a night, the second ending at 2:00 A.M. — there was not time or energy for attentive study or much spiritual activity.

"Here I go — I'm on," Gordon said. "I'll warm them up for you."

The Oak Ridge Boys came running off smiling, yelling, and clapping their hands. "It's a great audience, John. They're really *live* out there!"

The Oaks never cease to amaze me. They perform with such a fervor that every audience is the same. They exude the same joy on stage in Las Vegas as they would in a small-town, Alabama camp meetin'.

"Do you know that was the fiftieth show you've done with me here?" I asked them.

"Wow!" said Bill Golden of the Oaks. "Fifty times we've sung Jesus to that audience!"

"And you've 'sold' every time," I said. "Not many people can do that."

"It feels good out there," added Duane Allen.

"The feeling you guys produce feels good anywhere," I said.

I went onstage that night feeling pretty good myself, except for the built-in mechanism which made me want to be in bed at that time of the night. I decided to try and make this last show my best one if I could.

My opening song was *Ring of Fire,* followed by every song I've done in a concert over the last three years — *Sunday Morning Coming Down, I Walk the Line, These Hands, I Still Miss Someone, Peace in the Valley,* and *A Boy Named Sue.*

I had put together an "Americana Segment," featuring songs from our recent ABC-TV special "The Great American Train Story — Ridin' the Rails." This was like the "Ride This Train" segment we used to do on network TV and included such songs as *The Night They Drove Old Dixie Down, Mr. Garfield, Ballad of Ira Hayes, City of New Orleans,* and *Ragged Old Flag.*

Then on to a medley of up-tempo songs, railroad songs, with exciting lighting and visual effects: *Hey Porter,*

Folsom Prison Blues, Wreck of Old '97, and *Orange Blossom Special.*

I laughed and sang, fighting and denying the fatigue which was trying to pull me down. June joined me onstage, which, as always, brought my second wind and livened me up. Singing those songs like *Jackson* and *If I Were a Carpenter* with her seems to always come across "right."

Mother Maybelle came on after June and I did the duets. Las Vegas was her first performance since Pop had died. In introducing her, I said —

"She began her recording career in 1927. She, her brother-in-law A. P. Carter, and his wife, Sarah, were the original Carter Family. They recorded some 350 country, folk, and gospel song classics. She's a member of the Country Music Hall of Fame. Ladies and gentlemen, my legendary mother-in-law, Maybelle Carter."

I have never seen an audience that didn't love her. Vegas was no exception. She played the autoharp, one of her many instruments, and sang the timeless *Wildwood Flower* with such visible dignity and grace.

When Mother Maybelle finished her song, Anita Carter, our daughters Rosey and Rosanne, Gordon Terry, Jerry Hensley, and the Oak Ridge Boys joined me for the finale. We sang *Old Kentucky Home, Precious Memories, Will the Circle Be Unbroken?* and *Daddy Sang Bass.*

As an encore, the last song of the night was Arthur Smith's *The Fourth Man,* a rhythmic, exciting story-song about Shadrach, Meshach, and Abednego in the fiery furnace. The lighting gave the impression the whole stage was on fire.

With the song ended and the bows taken, I went back into the dressing room to rest. I didn't even have the strength to make it to my hotel room, at least for a few minutes. June and our friends and associates who arrange our personal appearances — Marty Klein of the Agency for Performing Arts and Lou Robin of Artist Consultants — sat down with me.

"It's 4:00 A.M. at home," June said. "Uncle Ermine Carter is getting up to milk cows and feed the chickens."

"Uncle Ermine doesn't have a contract with the Hilton," Marty quipped.

"And wouldn't want one," added Lou, laughing.

"When are we scheduled to come back here?" I asked.

"July and November of this year," said Marty. "Ten days each time."

"Oh, me," said June.

"Marty," I said, "if we could get the management here to agree, I'd like to postpone those dates."

I was thinking back to the soul-searching and promises I had made to myself in the hospital room following the jeep accident on Labor Day of the previous year — promises which had to do with slowing down.

"These Hilton people treat us like royalty," I said, "and I'll fulfill my contract with them. But the schedule is getting overloaded.

"I enjoy working in the showroom, and I'm pleased with what we've accomplished here. But I'd like to move those two ten-day engagements up to 1976 if they will agree," I continued. "It may sound selfish, but I think we're giving too much of ourselves here. I don't grow spiritually in Las Vegas. I'm barely holding my own, and I want to *grow*."

"Well, I'll talk with the entertainment director in the morning and we'll see," said Marty. "I surely understand. You aren't doing anyone any good if you kill yourself."

"If we can wait until '76 to come back, I'll be better prepared one way or another," I said.

"Prepared for what?" June asked.

"I don't know," I said. "But we've been coming here for three years, and we've proved everything we wanted to prove. And I keep remembering how you enjoyed that corn-on-the-cob at the Ohio State Fair and how we enjoyed the family audiences at some of the other fairs and one-nighters.

"Besides, I get behind in my homework and Bible study here, and when I'm out there traveling every day I can study on the bus or the plane.

"I don't agree with some people who say this is the devil's territory, because when God created the earth, He created Nevada, too. Anyway, the Spirit of God lives within you. And with all my new-found strength I believe I can keep my head and heart straight in Las Vegas or anywhere else. But — I just don't grow here, and I want to grow.

"And maybe if we wait until '76 we can make our return here a real event with the Bicentennial and all."

"Oh, boy," smiled June. "Tell that entertainment director I said 'pretty please,' and that I'll come dancing in on that stage singing a Bicentennial song!"

The next day I called home and talked with my mother. "I'm not coming home for a few days, mama," I said. "We're going to rest for awhile."

"What time did you finish up last night?" she asked.

"Two A.M.," I said. "Four A.M. your time, mama."

"No wonder you're run-down," she said. "That kind of life will kill you, son. You always get into trouble when you go against nature — and God is the Father of mother nature."

Mama was always quoting me something she had heard her daddy say when she was a young girl. And her recollections never failed to hold that gem of wisdom which she gleaned from living close to nature and close to God.

Marty Klein came in the room with a smile. "Your dates here at the Hilton have been moved up to July and November, 1976."

I breathed a sigh of relief. More time now for lots of things — *any*thing. Time and energy to write songs, to study, to record, some TV — possibly a series if we decide on it. Time with my family, time to take one day at a time so I can see where I'm going in this life. Time for whatever *He* wants me to do.

When Marty Klein left the room, I sat down and handwrote a letter to Billy Graham in which I said —

> ...June and I often talk about the week you and Ruth and your son Ned and nephew Mel spent with us Christmas last. We felt highly favored to be able to enjoy that much time with you. . . .
>
> If you remember, I asked you to consider coming to Las Vegas sometime this year while we're appearing here and see the show. . . .
>
> I know you are well aware of what particular stage of spiritual existence I'm currently in. I'm thankful I have gained at least enough wisdom to know that I'm not growing as well as I should be. . . .
>
> We won't be back here this year as I had told you previously. So I'll see you when I'm a guest on your Crusade in Jackson, Mississippi, in a few weeks. . . .

A few days later, we got home. It was time to go fishing again with John Carter. The sun was bright — a beautiful spring day — and we found our fishing poles and headed straight for the pond across the field.

We set out a catfish line on the bottom out in the middle, hoping to hang a big one. I had put some big catfish in the pond that spring. One of them weighed about four pounds, and we called him "Old Gray Whiskers."

We fished for a couple of hours while the afternoon sun dropped lower. We landed a bunch of perch, but the catfish line hadn't moved.

"We better go, son," I said. "Mama will be waiting supper for us."

John Carter said, "Daddy, let's leave the line out and maybe Old Gray Whiskers will get on it."

"OK," I said. "We'll come check it after supper."

When we sat down at the supper table, June gave thanks aloud. I gave thanks silently for the day, the boy, the home, and the lessons I'd learned.

I thought about adding, "And let Old Gray Whiskers get on that line while we're eating supper," but then I thought, "Better not approach God with some little selfish request like that."

But after supper when we got back to the pond, that line was straightened out and jerking like mad.

"You bring him in, son!" I said. "Pull! Pull!"

"He's too heavy, daddy! It's him! It's him! It's Old Gray Whiskers!"

It was him all right. When we got him on the bank, I knew he was that big one.

We put him on a stringer, and John Carter held one end and I held the other as we started across the field toward home.

"You know, son," I said, "I started to ask the Lord at the supper table to let Old Gray Whiskers get on the line."

John Carter had been as excited as I when we first caught him. Now he was silent, thinking about what I was saying, enjoying this special time together.

"But you know what, son?" I said.

"What, daddy?"

"I think the Lord put him on there because I *didn't* ask."

20 / **A Little Patch of Green**

I'd come in from California and had not even unpacked my bags when a call came from evangelist James Robison. His crusade was ending in Fort Worth, but if I'd come, they would extend it.

My mother had told me about James Robison, and after attending one of his services near Nashville, she had talked a lot about him to me.

When I told her that James had asked me to come to Fort Worth, my mother said, "You must go, son."

"I'm tired, mama," I said.

"The Lord didn't say it was going to be easy," said.

So that night I was in Fort Worth. It was a whirlwind trip, and early the following morning I was back on a plane from Dallas to New York, where I'd meet my family again.

We reached our cruising altitude of 35,000 feet, and I was thankful there were no clouds and the flight was so smooth.

I pushed the recliner button on the arm of the seat and laid back with my eyes closed, thinking about the service the night before.

My message to the crowd had been simple. I told them, "I'm not here tonight to exalt Johnny Cash or James Robison. I'm standing here as an entertainer, as a performer, as a singer who is supporting the gospel of Jesus Christ. I'm here to invite you to listen to the good news that will be laid out for you, to analyze it, and see if you don't think it's the best way to live."

Then I sang *Man in Black* and *I Walk the Line*. Then I talked about how I'd been a long-time-gone prodigal and about my coming back "home." I talked about the making of *Gospel Road* and about the songs that have been pouring out of me since I have been walking in the faith. I sang *Over the Next Hill, We'll Be Home*, and I closed with *Help Me*.

For fifteen minutes James Robison laid the gospel on the people and gave an altar call. About two thousand people responded to his invitation, and I stood over to the side and watched him receive those happy faces.

As I stood there watching James and the hundreds of people who responded, I thought about how he was different from other men — in front of a congregation or in private conversation. His only real interest was God and heavenly things.

"Why are men like Robison so bitterly criticized and abused by so many people?" I wondered. Why do so many nonbelievers think of them as some kind of freaks?

The answers came to me: They had been to the top of the mountain! They had seen heaven a little clearer than I had. Maybe things had been revealed to them that don't get passed around freely to the rest of us. The wind of the spirit had blown through their minds! That was it — the wind! The tree!

I thought of that old cypress tree standing alone in the bayou on the farm when I was a kid. The wind had twisted and torn its limbs and distorted its appearance. But it stood alone, its top touching heaven.

These men, these preachers whose voices touched millions — they look strange, sound strange to the world out there because they have seen farther from the top of the mountain. The wind of the spirit has given them an unworldly air. They are a rare breed.

The hum of those huge jet engines had me half-asleep as I shifted in my reclining seat. My thoughts raced back to my brother Jack and how he'd have loved being there the evening before. Those songs I'd sung for the people, how I'd joined in the chorus on *Just As I Am*. Wouldn't he have enjoyed that! I thought about my conversion when I was twelve. It was the same timeless peace I had felt the night before in Fort Worth.

And I thought about Jack on the night of my conversion. How he'd put his arms around me after I'd gotten up from that altar, the deepest show of emotion he had ever extended to me, I suppose. He was so strong, so tough. But he was so good. How important Jack had been to me in that relationship we'd found where there was so much love between us without ever having to say much about it.

Suddenly we hit a mighty bump — an air pocket — which knocked the coffee off everybody's table. I jumped up and looked outside. There still wasn't a cloud in sight. I couldn't see another plane or any other apparent reason for the disturbance. So I laid back, but there was a log in the pit of my stomach from the force of the impact.

I looked out the window again, and way off to my right was Memphis, Tennessee, about forty miles away. And then a chill went over me, because I knew *exactly* where we were. Straight down beneath me from that plane was a little patch of green — the Bassett Cemetery where my brother Jack was buried. Tears came to my eyes. From 35,000 feet, it was a postage-stamp-size patch of green, as straight down as I could look from the plane.

The instant we hit that bump, we had been directly over Jack's grave at Bassett, Arkansas.

I began to analyze how and why the bump we hit came about. But to me, there was no doubt in my mind why it happened. It was God's way of telling me I was on the right track. I was working toward what I was put in this world to do: entertain people; be something worthwhile to them; be an example; be a good influence; stand strong; don't compromise.

I really don't know what direction my life is going to take from here. I just know I'm on the track. Whatever He's got planned for me, I'm ready to listen. I'm ready to try to follow.

The bump was one of those beautiful "my cup runneth over" kind of blessings. It was a spiritual "high" which only comes once in a great while for me.

I looked down at that little cemetery plot fading back into the horizon, and I smiled and whispered, "Hey, Jack! I'm still singing those hymns you and I loved so much. I'll do a couple of them tonight on the show in New York.

"And by the way — I'll see you later, Jack."